Memories of The Indiana Soldiers and Sailors Children's Home

Arvine Ralph Curtis

Dedication

This book is dedicated to my homies, my virtual siblings with whom I grew up with in The Indiana Soldiers and Sailors Children's Home, and the dedicated staff of the home; our de facto parents.

Preface/Prologue

Each evening we go to sleep, our Guardian Angel on watch. Just before morning light we awake. We wave to thank our Angel for protecting us while we slept. We rise from natures beds and walk to the top of a hill. Side by side we stand, waiting for the sun to rise on the horizon. As it rises, it reveals an endless wasteland. We glance at one another momentarily. We grab ahold of the hands of our brothers and sisters next to us. We go together out into that vast unknown.

These are memories of life in a state institution for at-risk children. The memories recounted within are factual. Some details may have been omitted because of the time they happened and the time this story was said. These memories provide insight into the life in that institution. The author was sent to the institution at the age of four and graduated at the age of seventeen. After graduating, he worked at the institution while attending college. During this employment, he wrote many of the memories within this story. After relating these on a popular sharing media, he was encouraged to put them into print.

Table of Contents

1

Our Home

Those awful objectives of wars create victims. These victims are owed far more than can ever be repaid. Immediately after that war of wars, the state of Indiana recognized the debt owed to its veterans. It created a home that cared and provided shelter for the soldiers and sailors victimized by that war. Later the home cared for other victims of wars; the orphans of those whose sacrifices ensured our way of life. Appropriately, the home was named: *The Indiana Soldiers and Sailors Children's Home*. Still later, the home cared for at-risk children: victims of poverty, abuse, abandonment, and circumstance.

The home was nestled among a farming community, far from large cities and their seemingly inherent problems. The closest town was Knightstown, recognized now as the site of the Hoosier Gym. Many of those that maintained and cared for the children in the *Indiana Soldiers and Sailors Children's Home* raised their own children in that small town. The former *Indiana Soldiers and Sailors Children's Home* can easily be seen using popular software on the internet. From Indianapolis, go east on highway 40 to Knightstown. From there go south along highway 140 till you come to a large U shape building. That area is our home.

The home grounds could take your breath away. The grounds surrounded a small artificial lake, originally used as a water source for our ancient family. Once water was provided by other means, that ageless guardian changed the artificial lake into a natural lake. Surrounding the lake was luscious, well-kept lawns, well-trimmed bushes, and a variety of flowers. First generation trees sprawled over the grounds. Many with limbs larger than trees common of this era. One was a majestic matriarch settled in a beautiful valley: *Spring Valley*. She saw days when our Native Americans hunted for food. She grew to a height sufficient to oversee all for miles around. Among so many others at birth, she shot straight up in pursuit of that which gives life. Once free of the darkness, she spread her limbs and sent her children to take in that needed to grow. In return she gave what we needed to survive. When the home was established, she was joined by an old Civil War theatre; Lincoln Hall. They would remain companions for well over a century.

Lincoln Hall is a Civil War era theatre, now a historic landmark for that Hoosier state. A soldier and sailor dutifully stand guard over those within, immortalized on beautiful, stained glass windows as old and wonderful as the auditorium itself. Their constant vigilance reminds all within of the never-ending efforts of our veterans to guarantee that which we enjoy.

Nearly all needed to sustain the home was located on the home grounds. A coal power plant provided the utilities. A large farm provided milk and food. Food was prepared in a very large kitchen by dedicated cooks. Healthy diets were assured by a state a dietician. Meal time was probably the only time when one hundred percent punctuality was assured. Elementary and high school education was provided at Morton Memorial Schools, located on the home grounds. Children could further their education and attain skills from the many trade shops charged with maintaining the home. The farsightedness of those in charge of the home made these shops available to teach the children a trade. Their nearsightedness restricted most of these trades to the boys. The self-sustaining feature of the home was convenient, it also served to isolate the children from the real world.

An old brick structure, referred to as Town Hall, beckoned the children to come and play. Within her arms, the children participated in those age-old activities "girling" and "boying," bought candy from a small store operated by the children. A very old Wurlitzer juke box played the sounds of the big bands, and eventually the beginnings of rock and roll. Skills to realize that Hoosier dream were honed at the Town Hall gym. The gym was very small. The roof was so low that the ball would often get lost in the rafters. These rafters were considered in bounds. Subsequently, unique, comical passing and shooting strategies resulted. The hoops were much lower than regulation height, necessary because the roof was so low. The gym was so small that the walls served as out of bound markers. Proof of an out of bounds infraction could be often seen by the consequences of flesh meeting brick. The gym's hardwood floor randomly developed huge bulges, making dribbling an art in both dexterity and navigation. Regardless, a place to send a ball to the hoop is a beautiful place indeed for Hoosiers.

OUR FAMILY

Our home family began with the many people and organizations who recognized the debt owed to those that protected our freedoms; notably, the Grand Old Arm of the Republic, and the American Legion. Those that maintained the home and directly cared for the children became de facto parents. Civil War veterans and their orphaned children were the first to experience the love of the home. Finally, children that were victims from abuse, abandonment, and circumstance joined the family. Our family refer to the *Indiana Soldiers and Sailors Children's Home* as "the home", and to our virtual siblings as "homies."

SUPERSTARS

Many wonderful organizations volunteered their time, hearts and money for the children. The major sponsor was one made up of our veterans and their families, appropriately so for an institution with the name

The Indiana Soldiers and Sailors Children's Home. These superstars held special events, paid for various excursions outside the home, volunteered to take children on vacations during the summer, and made sure no child was forgotten on Christmas. Their only reward was that realized by most who sacrifice themselves to help those in need. Their efforts will forever be remembered in the hearts of those they ensured would not be forgot.

Visualizations and memories are constant companions. Sometimes these visualizations can take on a scary reality, given the right stage. Much later in life I took children to concerts. Together with our cotton balls, we oldsters opted to stay away from the floor next to the stage, where all the craziness took place. I found myself visualizing a very different scene than reality presented. The stage turned into an old farm; with an old farmhouse and large very old barn. It was a vision from memories of a time when a superstar family took me on vacation for a summer. The concert superstars changed into a lady, her husband, and three children. They made me one of their own for a summer. The children at the concert changed into my homies. Their craziness did not change. That visualization illustrated the superstar status of those that knew well that the love and care for children came first.

HOME STAFF

The home staff are constantly remembered in the thoughts and conversations of we homies. It is quite impossible for any rational adult to work at the home without developing fondness for the children. It is also impossible for the children to become fond of their caregivers. It was not in the interest of either to become too fond. I was told by one of the home staff that the most common reason for employee turnovers was because they developed to much of a fondness for the children.

During the time of this story, many of the home staff were World War II veterans. I believe the experience with the war made them ideally suited to provide guidance to the children. They never gave the impression they felt sorry for the children. They also were stark reminders to the children that the world in which they would eventually end up is not a rose garden.

One I lovingly refer to as the enforcer had considerable interactions with the children. A problem at any hour brought him to the scene. He was a strict disciplinary and quick to chastise those that were too sympathetic to their situation. Children regarded him highly. His efforts were more appreciated after they experienced life in the real world. I had the good fortune to work with him at the home after graduation. This friendship allowed me to gain some good perspectives on the home.

During the era of this story, the salaries for teachers at Morton Memorial High School were just about the lowest possible. Despite these low salaries, Morton had surprisingly many good teachers. It is a testimony that money itself cannot guarantee good teachers. I believe they were more motivated by the realization of improving the lives of at-risk children, rather than money.

Those best remembered by we children are those charged with our daily care; the governesses. They were the de facto parents. Each had to oversee twenty to thirty children 24/7. It gave a special meaning to that phrase "do not let them outnumber you." I simply cannot imagine how they managed to handle so many children! They must have been super humans.

RECOGNITION
Near the home is a quiet, secluded area, infiltrated only by the wind whistling through the surrounding trees. It is a resting place for our family that saw their worldly time come to an end while in the home. Many resting there are warriors of that war of wars. They returned from hell and were recuperating in the home when they joined their comrades that made the ultimate sacrifice. The home children knew well of their sacrifices. To prepare for that day dedicated to remembrances of our veterans, the children meticulously prepared that final resting place for a day of recognition. The grass hiding the monuments was cut. Insulting dirt was removed from the monuments. The monuments were then brushed lightly to reveal the identities of those resting there. Many had no identify. Each monument received fresh flowers, grown by the children specifically for this day. They placed a flag near each resting

place, surely to show those lying there that it still waved over the land of the free. On that day of remembrance, the children assembled their band and color guard. Every child marched to that resting place; the band playing that well-known refrain of Chopin, and the color guard carrying that symbol of what we pledge to defend. There they stood in silence as *Taps* was played and echoed from the woods surrounding the cemetery. It seemed as if the souls resting in that remote area summoned the children each year, urging them to remember their efforts, and that they also are members of the family from The Indiana Soldiers and Sailors Children's Home.

SURVIVAL

Children eventually must leave their home. Children who lived in the world that they must go are aware of what awaits. Many home children did not live in the world they would be sent. Contact with the world outside the home was not absent, but neither was it sufficient to effectively prepare the children for that which awaited them. Graduation was the gateway from the world of which they were accustomed, into a very different world. In a blink of an eye, children found themselves in this very different world. This necessitated adapting once again to a strange world. This abrupt change had to be traumatizing to some. One of my homes summarized it all too well "We all grew up again after leaving the home."

The sudden departure into the real world forced children to quickly devise strategies to survive. Their situations upon leaving their home initially was very different than most children experience. Most children outside the home usually had resources upon which they could depend to survive. Children leaving the home were promised a summer job, and a place to stay. After that job ended, they were on their own. Many were all alone. The children had to face that charging Rhino to survive. Many joined the armed forces. A few took advantage of the educational opportunities offered thru the state. Most relied upon their own devices and did the best they could. A few resorted to desperate measures. For a few, this sudden departure from their nest into a foreign world was too much to overcome. Knowing those difficulties our siblings faced, we homies cry for our brothers and sisters that did not survive, and for those that did. I saw education as the way to survive. After the first year of college I became familiar with some problems some of my siblings certainly faced.

2

Fate

Times and events are many times the product of well-designed plans. Those not planned are explained by a very creative term. Fate can be kind, difficult, or even terrorizing. It was all these as I journeyed to recall memories of life in the Indiana Soldiers and Sailors Children's home.

I was one of those homies that was ill-prepared for that world into which I was tossed. Immediately after leaving the home, I could never survive on my own. I depended upon a cousin with a heart too big. She had a family with its associated problems. Yet, she allowed me to share their lives. It will remain a debt that can never be paid. Motivated by that fear common for those whose roots are buried in poverty, I planned to survive thru education. I saved all the money I made that summer, and entered college. Not blessed with a keen mind, most of my time was spent at the library just to pass courses of which I had no interest. I got a job at the dorm cafeteria, cleaning the plates of food left over by the students. I never lacked a good meal. I worked at three jobs just to make ends meet. Unknowingly, I had done well to survive. I had attained a status that all children yearn: to become masters of their fate. I vowed forever more to be that master; to never again depend upon charity. It was a vow that could not be kept.

Few summer jobs were available after that first year of college. My lack of maturity and initiative ensured none would be. I swallowed my pride and again sought the kindness of my cousin. I hitched a ride to Indy where she lived. The next bus to her house was also the last bus for the day, about eleven-thirty at night.

As I boarded, the driver stopped me with a warning: "Son, you do not want to take this bus."

The peril in his voice warned me to take his advice. However, I had no choice.

He repeated his message and added, "It is for your own good." I still insisted. He muttered something to the effect "no one listens."

He asked me to sit at the front of the bus right behind him.

After a short ride, the bus suddenly stopped. Some boys were standing in front of it. They got on without paying. The bus driver never challenged them. Once they noticed me, they sat on seats on the other side of the aisle. They were intimidating, and offered some unflattering comments. Two got up and sat on both sides of me. They sarcastically complemented me on my attire. One branded a jackknife, waving it in some weird attempt to make sure I was aware of it. Attempts from the bus driver to intervene brought the attention of one of the bigger gang members.

The bus driver could only offer the words, "Be cool."

After making requests I could not refuse, they appropriated my Morton Memorial letter jacket, my shirt, and finally my new tennis shoes. I had to decide to fight back, or implement a strategy found necessary to avoid bullies while in the home.

Before I could put that plan into action, the bus again stopped. Two young, neatly dressed boys got on. They were paying customers. They had on black suits, black ties, and black shoes. Upon seeing these neatly dressed boys, some in the gang whistled. The two next to me immediately joined the other gang members on seats opposite the aisle. I could tell they were concerned. The neatly dressed boys surveyed this scene, surely noticing my lack of attire.

They asked "What is going down"?

The gang members' response was to immediately return my clothes. A motion of a hand from one of the two well-dressed boys was all that was needed for the gang to hastily make their exit.

A "thank you" to these neatly dressed boys only resulted in looks of disgust. They indicated that they did not do it for me. As they were getting off the bus, one turned to me. He told me something to the effect that I had better learn to take care of myself. After they left, the bus driver explained that those neatly dressed boys were followers of Malcolm X. The neighborhood was theirs, and they were angry because something had gone down in their neighborhood without their consent. The message from one of those neatly dressed boys that I should learn to take care of myself rang true. I became determined to do that rather than burden my cousin.

Efforts to take care of myself were laughable, at least nowadays. I quickly became companions with two friends always seen together; misery and disappointment. I became homeless. My brief experience in that status allowed me to gain greater appreciation for what we take for granted. Surprisingly, it was not hard at all to be homeless. As I recall, one dollar and sixty-nine cents was all that was needed to get a lot of those small hamburgers sold by a popular restaurant in Indy. There were plenty of strangers with "loose change" that were willing to help. Cleanliness was ensured thru the YMCA, who apparently never kept track of, or did not care, who used their showers. The *White River,* soap appropriated from the grocery store, and the heat from the sun proved beneficial to keep my clothes clean. The warm summer and the many parks ensured a secluded place to sleep. The threat of jail for loitering was common. Though not secluded, the large bus station in Indy was the favorite place when it rained. Of course, it does not rain in Indianapolis (LOL). I spent so much time at the bus station that I could recite the schedules in my sleep; literally. Humbleness was learned from the desperation brought about by hunger, and the ways it was dealt. I took drastic measures to avoid my homies when asking for change. While they probably would not recognize me, my Morton Memorial letter jacket was a dead giveaway.

I found myself next to a drug company's warehouse. I had worked there the previous summer, immediately after graduation from the home. I approached a stranger for some "loose change." He inquired about the Morton Memorial letter jacket I was wearing. After revealing I had earned it while in the home, he told me that his warehouse had previously hired graduates from the home for the summer. When I related that I was once one of those graduates in the previous summer, he gave me a couple of dollars, told me to clean up, and report to the warehouse the next day. I used the money for those little hamburgers at a popular fast food place. I cleaned up at the YMCA and reported to the warehouse the next day. This stranger took me into his office and phoned one at the home whom I fondly referred to as the enforcer. This enforcer arranged to give me a summer job at the home's paint shop, renovating some very old buildings. These buildings had seen little or no alteration since the time I was first admitted to the home. The journey through their chambers triggered memories of the times spent within. It was as if fate had by design forced me into a situation to remember my times and events in the home.

3

The Hospital

My first job that summer was to renovate the old hospital. This kind old structure was the first stop for children entering the home. There the children were checked to make sure they did not pose any danger to the home children. My perspective of this old structure as a young adult was very different than when I first visited as a toddler.

Each brick on this old hospital had aged differently. Each had its unique distortions, reflecting individuality we all seek. Vines were permitted to climb up to the roof of this old building, attesting to its age. Acid in those vines had etched perfect images of its leaves onto the thick, uneven, blue-tinged windows, as if to preserve its image for years to come. Refractions of the sunlight resulted in multi-color copies of images on the inside walls. It was a very colorful, consistently changing environment. Two stories and a large attic portrayed the building as gigantic to small children. Most of the building's interior was made of solid, thick wood, not veneered. The very tall, solid wood windows had very wide sills, enough to hold four of us small children. Solid wood floors spread out over the building, a feature common to all buildings at the home. Wooden stairs with very large hand rails led to a very long hallway with very large rooms on each side. The wooden floor and stairs objected when they were used, complaining that they were tired after all these years. What appeared to be very old candle holders transformed into electric lights struggled to provide sufficient light. In each room on both sides of the hallway were iron beds, lined up against the walls, exactly like one would witness in army barracks.

As I helped with the renovation of this old structure, I could not help to notice that the individuality of this old building was destroyed. Those wonderful, large, distinctive old red bricks were cloned by sand blasting. The vines were removed, as if to let the building know evidence of its age was unnecessary. The uneven, blue-tinged windows were removed, replaced by colorless glass of even thickness throughout. Gone were those multi-colored images, and the magic the images refracted into the building. It was as if the sole purpose of those new panes was to allow others to take notice of what was beyond them, ignoring their presence. The beauty of those solid wood floors was hidden with rugs. Insulting, prison-made paint hid the beauty of those wonderful wooden stairs and its hand rail. Participation in the distasteful work of destroying what it took a century to create would haunt me for years to come. As I revisited this old structure, I began to recall the events leading up to coming to the home.

4

Leaving Home

Making cookies was a favorite activity, and apparently one for Mom. It was important to make her happy. She often cried, seemingly for no reason. Rain on the previous night ensured ideal cookie dough. Also, Mom allowed me to use the kitchen, normally not allowed under any circumstance. The cookie dough was placed in the oven, and I pretended to cook them, just like Mom. I and the cookies made our way into the living room. We had a guest. Mom had taught me to be nice to guests. I and the cookies quickly made our way over her. Much to my dismay, she politely refused an offer for a cookie. More to my dismay, a cookie jumped off the cookie pan and onto her very shining shoes. She screamed, followed by one louder from Mom, then one much louder from the chef. Mom apologized to the guest but never scolded me. She escorted me to the bathroom, cleaned me up, and had me put on some clean clothes. Upon returning, Mom told me to say hi to a very nice person, which I did. I dutifully answered the usual rudimentary questions adults ask. After that useless interaction, she got down to the serious stuff. She asked if I would like to play with many other children my age. This sparked my attention! I glanced at Mom! She laughed and told me to answer. I did. The guest mentioned she knew where there were many other children my age, then suggested that perhaps we could go there sometime. I must have been fascinated with horses. I asked if there would be horses I could ride. She promised there would be. She left. Her next visit would be an unpleasant necessity.

PROMISES

When taken to the home, the promise there would be other children my age was to be. Not so for the promise there would be horses I could ride. This unfulfilled promise bothered me for years. Conversations with other homies revealed that similar, empty promises were made to them; usually when they were very young. Working at the home gave me an opportunity to inquire about these promises. I sought out the lady that had made the promises. She conveyed that children experienced considerable stress when taken from their parents. The very young were most vulnerable. To lessen that stress for them, a common strategy used by parents was used. Little white lies were told: carrot sticks that hopefully would lessen the stress of leaving their parents. One little white lie was the promise of horses and other animals. Upon hearing this, I had a different outlook on those promises. What strategies would you take to reduce the stress of children under similar circumstances? I found a deep respect for those people that had to remove children from their homes; especially the very young. Most of these young children could never comprehend the rationale for leaving the only home they knew. At least these people tried their best to lessen the stress.

LEAVING HOME

The day came when I and my three sisters had to say goodbye to our home and leave our loving parents. I know not how my parents said goodbye to my sisters. I know well how Mom said goodbye to me. Mom took me into the bedroom. She explained that I had to leave for a very long time. She said that I would be in a very wonderful home and "sises" would be with me. If I became scared, I should look for them. Mom's goodbye was very strange. She sang me a lullaby! She sang lullabies before, to put me to sleep. This lullaby was very different. The lullaby was about two little Babes, their names we do not know, who got lost in the woods a very long time ago. When night came, these two little Babes lay down to sleep. It was very cold, and the Babes cried. A guardian angel came, covered them with leaves to keep them warm, spread its huge wings, and watched over them as they slept. Mom told me to think of that lullaby and the guardian angel would come and stand over me. I left the only home I had known and my loving parents.

5

My New Home

fter Mom's lullaby, I was taken to the home. I do not remember my sisters being with me. It is hard to recall this time in my life. Most of the ride was filled with anticipation there would be what had been promised: i.e., other children to play with, and horses I could ride. After what seemed to be a short trip, we pulled into a driveway and stopped in front of a building that appeared to be an old church: Lincoln Hall. Our deliverer told us we would attend church there. A very large tree in a valley near this building caught my attention. The valley was named *Spring Valley*. Strangely enough, I felt a kinship with that tree. For the remainder of my life at the home I sat under that tree; reading or contemplating on the future. When it was cut down many years later, I realized the fate of the home would soon follow. We drove on, reaching an extremely large, fascinating building. It had more windows than could be counted, and very large pillars in front. We drove on, finally stopping in front of a huge brick, unassuming building. It was the same building that I helped renovate while working at the home. Children began home life in this hospital. It was distinguished by age and had the courage to accept any that needed its care. Those children that were found to pose no danger to other children were released into the company of their soon to be family.

For nearly a century this old hospital had seen so many pass through its chambers: victims of those awful objectives of war, orphans, the feeble minded, and children of neglect, abuse, abandonment, and circumstance. Certainly, it had long ago ceased to be surprised at their numbers and why they found their way in its arms. A lady dressed in white emerged. Her welcoming smile was desperately needed by children uncertain as to what fate awaited. Surprisingly enough, she called me by my name. She informed me that she had once taken care of Mom while she was sick. This revelation was most worrisome. I was not aware Mom had been sick. As we entered this old hospital, I and surely others asked that unanswerable question, "When can I go back home?"

We were led into a room where other children waited, on something or someone. Not one smiled. This triggered concern. I remembered Mom's instructions to look for "sises" if scared. As would be done many, many times; I looked but did not find them. With that instinct common to our species, I sought the comfort from an older girl. One by one, a girl briefly caught my eye, smiled, and quickly looked away, as if to indicate they had troubles of their own. One smiled and did not turn her head. I walked over and grabbed ahold of her leg; my guardian angel!

A nurse selected a child and led the child to a room across the hallway. Soon afterwards, we heard screams. This was repeated several times. I was terrified. When the nurse tried to take me, I tightened my grip on my guardian angel's leg. The nurse pried my hands loose and dragged me screaming over to that room. A man in a white vest stormed out, screaming about the lack of tools and the conditions under which he had to work. When he saw my terrified look, he quickly changed his demeanor. Adults are very good chameleons, changing demeanors on demand. A bribe of candy stopped the screaming, but not the concern. I was instructed to sit on this very large chair and open my mouth very wide. What followed is a memory embedded in my subconscious. I seem to have a dislike for dentists.

After this rather frightening unwelcome, we were led up a long wooden stairway leading into a hallway. Two very large dormitories were on both sides. Girls were sent to one dormitory and the boys to the other. It would be the last time brothers and sisters would share life together in the same living structures. Cast iron, military-style beds were lined up against opposite walls of the dormitory, exactly like one would witness in an army barrack. Permanent indentations in the mattresses attested to their ages, trapping the children as they slept. Though the beds were very small, no child fell out. A nurse ordered us to remove our clothes, put on gowns, and sit on assigned beds. We continued to ask the unanswerable question. Such sympathetic, giving persons, the nurses were overwhelmed by the sheer numbers that needed attention.

We were fed, with more food than I was used to. It was tasty, although without that flavor moms can provide. Remembering Mom's instructions to look for my sisters if afraid, I asked the nurse of their whereabouts. The nurse led me to the doorway, indicating they could be in the room across the hall. She explained it was against the rules to visit them. It would be the first introduction to the difference between the ivory tower rules, and those enforced by our caregivers. In plain sight of the nurses, I sneaked over to the girls' dorm across the hall. Bed by bed was visited, and sheet by sheet pulled to get the inhabitant's attention. After several attempts, one of the girls yelled that there was a boy wanting his sisters. Finally, I found a sister. I jumped onto the bed with her. The time together with a sibling would be the last for several years.

At bedtime, the nurse led me back to my bed in the other dormitory. We fell asleep; many crying. Occasionally, a nurse came in and gave water to the one crying the loudest, then tuck him in. I had to get in on that. We spent three days in this hospital being tested to make sure we would not endanger other children once sent among them.

6

Home Sweet Home

emories are hard to recall in their correct timeline. My job
at the home helped in that respect. My first job was to renovate the hospital, the first building that welcomed me when
entering the home. The second job was to paint bathrooms in Division
30, the second building that welcomed me. It was as if something or
someone was forcing me to relive the events of many years ago, in the
timelines they occurred.

Our time in the hospital came to an end. We had been tested and
found adequate to join our family in the home. We were led down a
cement walkway alongside huge brick buildings. Older girls sitting on
extremely large cement porches in front of those building welcomed us
with smiles and the usual rudimentary questions. Their welcomes were
most comforting. They distracted from concerns of being in a strange
place, not knowing what would befall us. We stopped in front of one of
these brick buildings. The girls were instructed to remember the number 31, and the boys the number 30. These would be our new homes.
Remembering only a number for my home seemed so strange. Mom

tried to have me remember our address, which certainly was not so simple. Each living quarter in the home was referred to as a division. Each division was identified by a unique number and dedicated to a specific age group. Division 30 was reserved for boy toddlers, and Division 31 for girl toddlers.

Children were quickly introduced to a facet of home life much different than what they were accustomed with parents. They were separated into groups, determined by sex, age, and something related to toughness. Each group lived in separate housings. They would remain together for their entire life in the home. Mothers' instincts are to keep their children together. Subsequently, all children of a family would find themselves in the home. Because of the groupings, siblings would never again share the daily comfort and companionship from those which they were accustomed. Though living apart, they could renew their companionships during playtimes and planned activities.

Upon entering Division 30, I came upon what was promised; other children, all my age. More surprising was that they were all boys! Coming from a family of four sisters, I always wanted a brother. But so many? They were playing, seemingly free of concerns. One of them jumped up, grabbed my hand, and took me back to others that were playing together. Another handed me a toy, and we started playing. Another warned me to avoid talking to one of the governesses, as she always got mad. These children did not seem to suffer the concerns that I did. They appeared anxious to welcome me into their fold. It was as if they sensed my suffering and wanted to provide comfort.

GOOD COP/BAD COP

Parents probably believe they have well-thought-out strategies in dealing with their children. What strategy would you use for a family of about thirty? Think about it! Our two governesses employed the good-cop, bad-cop strategy. After a few weeks, we knew them both as good cops.

There were three set of rules in the home. There were the ivory towers. We children only knew those that the governesses enforced. They were much less restrictive than those ivory tower rules. We children had our own rules. Arrival of new children triggered a ritual; the reading of the rules the governesses enforced. We were led upstairs to a very large dormitory. The cast iron beds with their captive mattresses were lined up, exactly like those in an army post. We were instructed to stand by our beds. The child who had first welcomed me grabbed my hand and took me to a bed adjacent to his.

Like an army sergeant, the bad cop barked out the rules. Occasionally, she reminded us of the punishment that awaited those who did not obey. Strangely enough, she looked directly at the same child on each reminder. The first rule was that our beds were now our rooms. We were to place all that we owned under our beds, oops, I mean our rooms. She added that no one could touch stuff under another's room. She continued with the expected rules: no biting, hitting, and so on. She emphasized the most important rule; to not bother the governesses once they retired for the night. Shoes could not be worn inside the building. One of my newfound *friends* saw fit to point out I violated this rule. Thank a lot! Others quickly pointed out several other violations; prompting crying. The bad cop barked even louder, ordering me to stop crying and act like a big boy. I became so upset that I lost control of a certain and necessary bodily function. The consequences ended up on the floor, initiating more and louder crying. The bad cop repeated her scolding while the good cop consoled me. I learned quickly not to displease the bad cop. My ordeal with the rules continued.

NUMBER ONE AND TWO

Sharing the bathroom certainly is a problem for families with more than one child. With thirty toddlers, one bathroom, and only two toilets, think about it! This necessitated a strategy for using the bathroom. We were led into the bathroom. Two toilets were on raised platforms, with long narrow rugs in front, giving meaning to that saying, "The king's throne." The bad cop explained that one toilet was to be used only for number one, and the other only for number two. The other children seemed to have understood the meaning of number one and number two. Some lined up. Number one and two were not the choices I had learned. Mom and Dad referred to these as pee and poop. To avoid the bad cop's wrath, I pretended to know what number one and two meant. I lined up with other children in front of a toilet. When my turn came, I sat down on the toilet to poop. The children in the line behind me started screaming, holding their privates. Although well familiar with that language, it was too late! I had started to squeeze one out. Trust me, when other children scream at you, you quickly learn the rules. The good and bad cops laughed, then came over and scolded me. I had to learn the ones and twos of going to the bathroom.

LEVERAGE

Emphasize was placed on the most important rule. Our governesses could never be bothered after they retired for the night! Violation invited a threat to be spanked. My interpretation of the bathroom rule was that permission had to be granted. I noticed other children breaking that rule. The possible wrath of the bad cop ensured that I would not. Permission was always sought.

One night after the governesses had retired, the immediateness of my need called for quick action. Several knocks on the good cop's door brought no response, as did knocks on the bad cop's door. However; her door was partially open. With more courage than a child should have, it was pushed open. Calling her name also brought no response. I entered, and heard sounds emanating from under the blanket, much like Dad made. I shook her. She lifted her head and grouchily asked what I wanted. Running first entered my mind, but it was more important to go to the bathroom than experience her bluff to spank me. After asking permission, she grouchily told me permission was not needed to go to the bathroom. She turned over, then warned me not to bother her again. Before leaving, I noticed a smell much like that of Dad when he came home late. I told her that I hoped she would not get into trouble like Dad did when he came home late smelling like that. She hopped out of bed and grabbed me by the shoulders. Looking straight in my eyes, she made me promise never to tell anyone about that smell. After that experience, both governesses were very good cops.

7

Coping and Adapting

While working at the home, I stayed in an apartment on the home grounds. After work, I participated in that age-old activity. Lake Graham had more blue gills than can be imagined, and bass large enough that a fisherman could lie without being embarrassed. One of the best spots for bass to hang out was below rock-built steps leading into the lake behind Division 30. Spring water flowed down those steps into the lake. Underneath those steps bass waited for whatever washed their way. After no success fishing that spot, I sat down to rest on the lake bank next to a large tree. I experienced a feeling of déjà vu. I realized I was sitting in the same spot that I had spent many hours while a toddler in Division 30. This triggered a long-forgotten memory of my efforts to cope from being taken from my parents.

With so few governesses to help, most children were left to their own devices to cope with the sudden changes in their lives. Older girls living next to our building set their own problems aside to help. As strange as it may seem, other toddlers also helped. Something forced me to ignore the pleas of the older girls and my friends to play. I chose to sit on the bank beside Lake Graham. It was the exact spot where I was resting from fishing. There I watched fish do whatever fish do, listened to frogs at dusk, and watched large, scary snapping turtles appear and quickly disappear. Sitting alone by this lake gave me time to dwell in that hope of hopes; that my parents would soon come to take me home. It may be foolhardy to believe something will come true if you wish hard enough. However, consequences of desperation can be very strange. Mom actually came!

Mom sang that lullaby! Her voice was as clear when I first heard it. Initially it was scary to hear from my Mom when I realized she was not there. In time that fear was replaced by the comfort of her voice. I became addicted to that intoxicating comfort. For many weeks, my only agenda was to sit on the bank and wait for Mom. The words from that lullaby generated a vision of a guardian angel protecting me. Although only a vision, it was very real in my mind, and very comforting. I wondered if my sisters were also protected. This strange behavior did not go unnoticed by the staff. They arranged for me to go see Mom!

SEEING MOM AGAIN

The trip to see Mom was not that long. The car pulled up to a very large building, within which were people wearing mostly white clothes. The nurse gave stringent instructions not to touch Mom. I was led to a room where I saw Mom lying on a bed. The bond between a child and a mom are much stronger than any instruction on how to act. A run followed with a leap found us hugging as if we had not seen each other for some time. Much later in life, Mom told me that she had hardly gotten a word in. A memory best remembered was a question most homies asked themselves, and wanted to ask their parents. "Why was I sent to the home"? I asked Mom that question. She avoided that answer.

Much later in life, at about the age of thirteen, the state decided it was not necessary to quarantine her. They allowed me to go on vacation with my parents during the summer. It would be an enlightening summer. I asked Mom about the decision to place us into the home. As difficult it surely is to realize your children can no longer live with you, enough courage must be gathered to make tough but necessary decisions. Mom first considered our relatives. Some failed the parent test. Some had children and problems of their own. Some indicated they would take one, only one. This was not an option. An instinct of mothers is to keep their children together. Mom discovered that her distant relatives faced the same decision. They placed their children in *The Indiana Soldiers and Sailors Children's Home*. To keep us together, Mom made the same difficult decision. She started to cry as she told me this. I hugged her and ended that conversation. Recalling some life experiences extract too much of a price.

When it was time to leave, Mom told me she would always be there, thinking of me and *sises*. She made me promise to play with the other children. Right before leaving, she asked if I remembered the lullaby and the guardian angel. I sang her the lullaby. Much later in life, Mom explained that she had been pleasantly surprised that I had remembered that song, as she had sung it to me only once. Mom told me to remember the guardian angel and not forget about *sises*. We said goodbye again, only this time for a very long time.

NIGHTS AT THE HOME

I arrived back at the home very late at night. The children and home staff had gone to bed. The cab driver let me out at the end of the long walkway leading to my division. He instructed me to go to my *home*, and drove away. The shadows from a full moon threw different perspectives on the surroundings than what daytime shed. Their enchantments lured me in their direction, away from my division. The lake was a mill pond, perfectly mirroring the surroundings reflected by the moonlight. While gazing on these perfect reflections, the noise of a waterfall got my attention. I discovered water disappearing over what seemed like a bottomless pit. A fence much higher than I protected the children from falling into that pit. It also prevented me from seeing what was at the bottom. I climbed the fence to get a better look. At the bottom of the pit was a tunnel. I bent over further to see into the tunnel. I found myself at the bottom of that waterfall, soaking wet. I sat there for what seemed like an eternity, crying out to those not there. I eventually gave up.

Curiosity can be very dangerous, yet very rewarding. I decided to see where this tunnel led. By this time, my eyes had adapted to the dark. I could easily manage the large cement blocks inside the tunnel. About halfway thru, I heard what sounded like water trickling in a brook. I also noticed subtle light in the distance. I went towards the light. I exited the tunnel and came upon some very large stones, arranged to guide the water into a small stone-lined brook. The exit was well hidden by tall evergreen trees. It would be one of my popular dating spots much later. The stone surface was slippery. I found myself sitting in that small brook.

After meandering alongside the brook for a distance, I realized that I was in a very large valley. I climbed up one side of the valley, coming upon a cement walkway. It was well hidden by pine trees alongside the valley. It was a very strange place for a walkway, leading nowhere but to a very large pine tree. Later that pine tree became known to me as a sweetheart tree. I kissed my prom date under that tree. Exiting this walkway, I came upon a very large building. It was the same building I saw upon entering the home; the one with more windows than be counted. The entrance had extremely large pillars on both sides. I created this fantasy of a castle. I made my way past the two very large pillars and encountered very large double doors, exactly like one would see on a castle. Attempts to open those heavy doors were futile. Just as I was about to give up, one door swung open and a man walked right by, unaware of my presence. I quickly made my way inside before the door closed. The castle had a very high ceiling, causing me to lose focus on where I was going. I tripped on a steep, very wide stairway. Curious as to where that stairway led, up the I went.

Several locked rooms accomplished what they intended to do. One not locked resembled the bedroom of a queen. Her extremely large bed was under a canopy lined with white fluffy material, exactly like what we saw in movies of old England. On the bed was huge pillows and silk sheets. It was fun rolling around and bouncing on that very soft mattress. I left it and the blankets wet and disordered.

After being challenged with what all children avoid, I left the Queen's room. I ventured down a very long hallway, leaving the building via an outside stairway. I came upon a small park, known as the Jack and Jill park. In the center was a familiar cement pool in which we toddlers wadded on summer weekends. The pool was empty, but the faucet easily managed. After some time stomping in the water, I realized one of the home staff watching. I later would find out he was superintendent of the home. He must have asked the usual questions. I cannot recall. Regardless, he took my hand and led me back to the walkway leading to my division. He let loose of my hand and like the cab driver, instructed me to go to my division. While he watched, I made my way down that long walk back to my division. Upon reaching the division, I tried to open the door. I could not open it! I looked back for the superintendent. He had left for his home, close by. Not a problem! I made my was to my favorite place by the bank. I curled up with my coat and fell asleep, waiting for Mom's lullaby.

WHERE IS YOUR CHILD

I was awakened in the early morning by a commotion. The superintendent and governesses were on my Division's porch, yelling at each other. As they focused their attention on each other, I walked by unnoticed. It was a special day. Pancakes were being served. While we were about to make short work of those pancakes, those responsible for the commotion entered, still yelling at each other. A child was missing! Extremely upset, the governesses told the superintendent he should have made sure the child was inside the division. The good cop told the superintendent to search the lake, since that was where he spent most of his time. Kevin, sitting next to me, realized who they were talking about. He asked why they had to search for me, since I was sitting next to him. The adults turned towards me, certainly astonished that I was there. They looked at each other momentarily and started to ask me questions Those questions were ignored. There were pancakes to be had. Dealing with so many children, surprises such as this, and the subsequent astonished looks, would be repeated often. Maybe that would explain why one of the governesses smelled like Dad.

ADAPTING

I continued to ignore the pleas from the older children and my brothers to play. I sought my favorite spot next to the lake, and waited for Mom's lullaby. The child who had first taken my hand upon entering Division 30 joined me. Little attention was paid to him. Mom's lullaby was far more important. One of the girls, probably his sister, occasionally came and sat with him for a while. After some conversation, she gave us both a kiss on the cheek and left. After Mom sang her lullaby, the ducks were fed, complements of bread provided by the governesses. We then stimulated our curiosities, asking ourselves questions, such as; why do fish live in water, what are those strange sounds made in the evening, and many more. On hindsight, this must have been our way of coping.

With each visit to the lake, Mom's voice came later and later. Each time it faded more and more. In time, her lullaby was no more. We continued to go to that special place, now only to feed the ducks and play together. Each day, the sounds of the other children and older girls playing became louder, drawing our attention. Remembering the promise made to Mom, I said goodbye to the ducks, grabbed the hand of my companion, and we went to join the other children. Upon seeing us approach, the other children welcomed us with cheering. I wonder if that welcome meant they were glad we had survived an ordeal such as they had also experienced, and were now part of their family. Although I played with the other children, I occasionally would visit that place by the lake, trying to recreate that time when Mom sang that lullaby.

HOPE OF HOPES IS JUST THAT

The suddenness of leaving loved ones, and living without them, surely had a lasting effect on children. One hope most young children held onto for years was that their parents would soon come to get them. It must have been extremely difficult for the children to deal with this. It also was difficult for the governesses. Knowing it was extremely unlikely this hope would be realized, and probably the only hope the children had, just how would you address their questions? Could you destroy that one hope? The governesses chose not to; at least when we were very young. When asked the question, it was not answered. It became the unanswerable question. Later children realized that the hope of hopes was just that. It would take an act of disobedience and punishment to make me realize that.

My job working at the home provided the opportunity to recall that moment. I was ordered to replace a window in Division 9. This window was right above a spot where the punishment chair resided. It was a chair I knew ever so well. As I worked on replacing this window, I saw a vision of that moment when I once occupied that chair.

Division 9 was right next to Divisions 10 and 11. These divisions were homes to girls and boys of the same color, and all ages. The punishment chair was right next to a window, in plain view of Division 10 where the girls lived. I had been punished for the umpteenth time, of course for something I did not do. Time on the punishment chair gave me plenty of time to dwell on that hope of hopes. While gazing out the window, a girl ran out of Division 10. She sat on the porch, sobbing.

Her governess yelled, "Your parents will never come to pick you up. The sooner you realize that, the better off you will be."

The governess then sat beside the girl, putting her arm around the girl's shoulders, mumbling something that sounded like "lordy, lordy, lordy." Words meant for others can have profound effects on unintentional listeners. I realized that my hope of hopes was just that.

For myself, that hope of hopes turned into fantasy. Fantasy may be worse than hope, but it is much easier to manage. The reality I would stay in the home allowed me to focus on my life at the home, rather than fantasy. Understandably, the hope of going back home seemed to be a common theme of the children. Even after realizing it was fantasy, they still held it close to their hearts. I still cry when I hear that song in a movie where a girl was taken from her loving family to a strange world. She also posed that unanswerable question in a song. When the home ceased to exist, many of the children attempted to preserve that which they knew as their home. The theme song for the home's museum reflected that hope of hopes.

8

Chosen Ones

Summer ended, and so did my job at the paint shop. While waiting for a ride back to college, I heard toddlers screaming in glee. Those sounds were complements of toddlers splashing in the cement wading pool in the center of the Jack and Jill park. When the toddlers came to splash in that small pool, many of the home staff gathered and looked on. This scene reminded me of the time when I was one of those toddlers.

CHOSEN ONES

Causes for being placed in the home were blind to all that made children different, the exception possibly being poverty. We lived, slept, ate, and played with children of different ethnicities, backgrounds and just about all that makes us different. We children recognized these differences only for what they were. It was an invaluable lesson. To this day, I feel sorry for those who read into these differences other than what they are.

While we children ignored differences, the older girls and the governesses certainly did not. It did not go unnoticed that some of my siblings were consistently chosen first by the older girls to play. Some even had girlfriends. Also, the governesses seemed to favor certain children. These children were the chosen ones, literally. With so many children and so few adults, there was considerable competition to get your fair share of attention; unless you were a chosen one.

Desperate to get my fair share of attention, I mimicked one of the chosen ones. He appeared to get more than his fair share. The consequences taught me a very valuable lesson. Every Saturday, during the summer, we toddlers splashed in this small, cement wading pool at the Jack and Jill park. Adults gathered around the pool to watch. When one did something cute, they would laugh and point to the fortunate one. This attention did not go unnoticed by the other toddlers. We tried our best to outdo the others to gain attention. Jumping in feet first was common, which all of us did, coming up to see if the adults were watching. He whom I tried to be was extremely competitive. To get attention he jumped into this shallow pool belly first, bringing oohs from the adults. You could see the joy on his face from the attention he was getting. Well, this was my chance to show I was also there. I yelled for the adults to watch, then dove in head first! The encounter between the cement bottom and flesh turned the water a scarlet red. I am not sure how the adults reacted. I was busy crying. The sight of blood surely drew different reactions than oohs. It certainly emptied the wading pool. In their usual directness, my governesses tried to introduce me to that characterization *stupidity*. Some lessons we learn the hard way. I decided at a very young age that duplicating others must be done with discretion.

WHAT!

After several times of not being chosen, we "unchosen ones" skipped the selection process. We went our own ways. Realizing some children would be chosen over others was an introduction to the reality that perceptions of children can create distinct groups, at least in the minds of the adults.

Much later in life, I realized that the chosen ones were the cute ones. I was not cute? There must be some mistake!

THE LITTLEST THIEF

One chosen one, or cute one if you wish, proved to be an interesting Grinch. At Christmas in Division 30, those with parents received a toy truck or car. Those without parents received the same, from sponsors who made sure no child was forgotten. We were instructed to keep our toys in our rooms; that is, under our beds. The morning after Christmas, every toy was under the bed of our tiny Grinch! When we went to get a toy, this tiny Grinch screamed that it was his. The governesses realized it was inappropriate to allow him to get away with stealing. They ordered our tiny Grinch to return the toys. He was a very busy boy that night, trying to find out whose toy was whose, and returning them.

ONCE A THIEF

Children change considerably over the years, some for the better, a few for the worse. Some characteristics seem to follow them forever. Our littlest thief came to the home believing what was his was his, and what was ours could be his. Later in life, he seemed to retain this philosophy. He was the top dog of cuteness, very tender, and likeable child. He also was a very good friend. He left the home for a few years. He returned; a very different and very tough child. Although he was our age, he was appropriately placed in a division with older children.

At this age, we all had our own lockers, like the ones seen in schools. Many did not bother with locks, probably because there was nothing worth stealing. Those believing they had something worth stealing bought cheap locks from the five and ten cents store at a nearby town. Almost all obtained a lock right before Christmas time. It was that time when some of the more unscrupulous children thought to improve their holdings. About a week after Christmas, our possessions disappeared, despite our locks. I remembered when this littlest thief had taken the Christmas presents. Evidently, he added to his expertise the art of picking locks. Fortunately, one of my friends was by far the master at that.

He was easily bribed to pick the lock of our littlest thief. The locker was full of our possessions! I waited for the littlest thief to return. I very carefully pointed out that he had stolen our stuff. He became very upset and threatened me with physical violence if I told. I was afraid and at the same time disappointed. Afraid of getting my butt kicked, and disappointed he thought I would tell. We children never told, never! I told him that he should return the possessions. I realized that he would never do that. Miracles do happen. As he had done years before, he was a very busy boy that night. Perhaps he remembered that Christmas when we were very young.

9

Times and Events in Division 25

One of the most enjoyable jobs while working at the home was renovating Division 25. Like the old hospital, Division 25 was a majestic old building, built in the late 1800s or early 1900s. It was home to kindergarten and first grade children. Two very tall, wonderful, solid-wood double doors guarded the entrance to Division 25. They were so heavy that we smaller children had to wait for one of the larger kids to pry one open. The windows were beautiful, built of solid wood, about six to eight feet high with arches. The uneven, blue-tinged window panes shared the same character as the old hospital. The ceiling in the living room was decorated with hypnotizing images, painted by old masters of that trade long forgotten. Just about every day we lay on small rugs in the living area to take a nap. It provided opportunities to view the creations of those masters. It was akin to looking at cloud formations and liking them to images which we were familiar. The ceiling of this division had never been touched over the twelve years of my stay at the home. I recognized many images! When I first approached Division 25 to begin with the renovation, I saw several little red wagons lined up

· under the outside stairs leading to the dormitory. It triggered a recall of a special time when we moved from Division 30 to Division 25.

MOVING

Great pains were taken to separate boys and girls. Their living quarters were placed on opposite sides of Lake Graham, or far from one another. Fortunately, this kind old lake never objected to an occasional crossing. Of course, out of sight of those who oversaw the children. Forever more at the home, the way of life would be boys living only with boys, and girls only with girls. None would be their siblings. How this affected the children, or even if it affected the children, is unknown. Certainly, the girls reveled by the fact they would have so many sisters, and no brothers. The same for the boys; many brothers and no sisters. I say that with tongue in cheek of course.

Each group lived together in a separate building, referred to as a division. They ate together in one large dining room, played together on the same playground, slept together in one large dormitory, and went to planned activities together. This togetherness cultivated lifetime kinships. They became virtual siblings. Each year, children of a specific age group moved to another division with a different governess. This separation from those they depended upon benefited the children and the governesses. After all, familiarities are seeds for love and contempt. It was not in the best interests of the governesses and the children to share too much of either.

Divisions 30 and 31 were reserved for preschoolers. They were on the same side of the lake that girls lived. Boys old enough for kindergarten were transferred to Division 25. Division 25 was across the lake, where the boys lived. To help transport our possessions, big hearts in an organization sponsoring the home bought each of us a little red wagon. I said that correctly! They bought each of us a red Radio Flyer wagon! We said goodbye to the good cops and the older girls. I and my companion advised the ducks we would be across the lake. With our possessions in those little red wagons, we made our way across the lake to Division 25. While most did not need a wagon, the littlest thief's wagon was packed so high that a couple of us had to walk alongside it to prevent it from tottering over. I missed the older girls who played with us. They had given much needed comfort. Fortunately, Division 25 was directly across the lake from the older girls' divisions, well within sight. Sometimes, we would gaze across the lake in attempts to see our Guardian Angels.

EXPECTATIONS

Those Guardian Angels had been sources of our games before moving to Division 25. Without them, we relied upon our own imaginations. With twenty to thirty imaginations, there were no shortages of games. Most games were molded after old black and white movies of pirates, Tarzan, cowboys and Indians. Most wanted to play the part of a cowboy. I was no `exception. One child in our division was a Native American. We met under a stairway of Division 25, and made a promise to be friends for life. We kept that promise. After that promise, I never played the role of a cowboy again. Playing the part of an Indian introduced me to what can happen when children's expectations are severely altered.

After a very trying game of being shot several times by cowboys, my Native American friend took me aside and explained that the Indians did win sometimes. Upon asking my governess about this, she related the battle of Little Big Horn, known as Custer's Last Stand. In our next game, when the cowboys shot us Indians, we did not die! The cowboys were told that in this battle, the Indians won and the cowboys had to die. Some cowboys yelled that we were not playing right, some looked at one another in disbelief, some quit the game, some died with reluctance, and some even joined our side. I guess extreme changes in children's expectations have strange consequences, and everyone likes a winner.

TRAINABLE

The home could have served well as a classroom to train child psychologists. I had taken college classes in psychology. While working at the home, many parallels were witnessed between what I learned from that class and what was exhibited by the children. One obvious parallel was between a theory by some dude called Ivan, and a strategy adapted by the home to control the children. Ivan confirmed that dogs could be conditioned to react in a specific way; simply by the sound of a bell. As every dog owner knows, the dogs had to be rewarded when acting appropriately, using dog threats. The home implemented Ivan's theory, using a whistle in place of a bell. It was a very loud and annoying steam whistle, one that could be heard for miles. Substituting for the dog treats was the *reward* of not being punished. I never realized the effectiveness of Ivan's strategy; at least until I attempted to leave a psychology class.

During the psychology class, an extremely loud steam whistle was heard, complements of the power plant at the college. Coincidently, the college had the same whistle as the home, with the same annoying sound. Upon hearing this whistle, and to the surprise of the professor and my classmates, I calmly gathered my books and proceeded out of the classroom. The professor stopped me and asked why I had to leave at that specific time. Waking up from some strange trance, I told him a lie. The truth was that I had been trained by the home to react to whistles, true to the theory by Ivan. It might seem sick to train children using whistles, but it proved effective.

THE WHISTLES

A problem haunting the management of large groups of people is how to make sure they perform certain activities, and are at the same place, at specific times. The ivory tower people found a solution, adapting Ivan's strategy. At pre-school ages, we were told to ignore frequent, loud, and annoying whistles. In Division 25, we evidently were old enough to be trained. The governesses conveyed the meaning of each whistle and what to do when we heard them. After twelve years hearing and being conditioned by those whistles, their meanings are still all too well known. Now keep with me on this; it gets sort of muddled, confusing, and probably unbelievable.

A whistle at about six thirty in the morning signaled the children to wake up. It was a very useless whistle indeed. Fifteen minutes later a whistle warned the children they absolutely had to be out of bed. This was not a useless whistle. Ignoring it could find oneself sitting on his butt next to his bed. The next whistle signaled the children to get ready for breakfast, perhaps to wash their hands. It had a very different meaning to many children. Right before each meal, the governesses left to eat, leaving the children alone for about a half hour. Many children took advantage of this opportunity to go elsewhere. That wash-your-hands whistle warned them to return before the governesses conducted a head count. The seven o'clock whistle signaled the children to go to the dining hall for breakfast. It was one whistle that no child was ever punished for disobeying. Not so for the next whistle, about forty-five minutes later. It signaled them to get ready for school. Fifteen minutes later, yet another whistle signaled them to go to school. Now, this description of the whistles may seem unbelievable to you *non-homies*. I assure you it is true, very true. Near noon, a whistle warned the children to be in the division and to prepare for lunch. As mentioned before, it also served as a warning they had to return from wherever before the governesses conducted a head count. Fifteen minutes later, another whistle signaled them to march over to the eating place for lunch. After lunch, a whistle signaled them to go back to school. At supper time, a whistle instructed them to get ready for supper, followed with the usual whistle, "Get back to the division before the governess conducts a head count". Later, a whistle signaled the children to march over to the dining hall for supper. In the evening, around nine, a whistle told the children to go to bed. At ten, another warned them that they absolutely had to be in bed. I believe there was a whistle at about ten thirty, although by then I was usually asleep, unless there were plans for the night. Now, I bet some families would love to implement this whistle scenario. Trust me; your children will hate you.

SKATING LESSONS

While renovating division 25 during my summer job, we removed the furniture and rugs, in preparation to sand the oak hardwood floors. We found they were in unbelievably good condition, despite their century old age. I explained why to those with whom I worked.

All the old buildings at the home had beautiful, thick, solid hardwood floors, not veneered. To keep us busy, and at the same time maintain the beauty of those floors, the state implemented a very good training program for skating. Wax was spread on those hardwood floors and thick cloths attached onto our feet. We skated around the floor, making it mirror shiny. We referred to this appropriately as *rub-coating*. The skill used to rub-coat was the same used for skating. Most of home children became very good skaters, the wheel kind. Once the floors were thoroughly waxed and slick, they were put to good use, such as jumping on those cloths and seeing who could slide the furthest.

MEMORABLE MOMENTS

While renovating Division 25 during my summer job at the home, I mentioned to the governess there had to be many problems trying to oversee so many children. She agreed there were many problems. However, she told me something that every parent realizes. These problems later become memorable moments. The more children there were, the more problems, oops, I mean memorable moments. Parents have a few children from which these memories originate. Governesses had several hundred children, and consequently thousands of memories. I enjoy the homecomings when we children relived life in the home. I believe that when these governesses got together, there were many more memories recalled and enjoyed. I will narrate some of my most memorable moments while in Division 25.

NECESSITIES

To make one memory appreciated, one should know about the clothing situation in Division 25. We were all provided very heavy, scratchy wool underwear and socks, complements of the penal system. They were discarded at the first opportunity. Cherished was a pair of farmer-style trousers with buckled straps, very large front and back pockets, and two side pockets. They could store lots of junk. There were plenty of other clothes from parents or sponsors of the children. One very large closet held these clothes. Each child had a two by two bin to hold their own clothes. These bins were on shelves, each attached to the other. Additionally, there were shelves to hold the bed sheets, winter coats, boots, and other necessities. With about twenty to thirty children, there was a mountain of clothing in that closet. I got to know how much, complements of a very strange game.

THE COCKROACH GAME

Division 25 was next to the shallow end of Lake Graham, home to very large water bugs. They were completely harmless and apparently somewhat tasty. These bugs were lovingly referred to as cockroaches, probably because that seemed to instill fear into the hearts of the home staff. They did not need to worry about cockroaches. These water bugs were so large and numerous that no smart cockroach would dare stick around. For that matter, I cannot recall any mice either. I may be joking about that! Now that I think about it, there were no mice!

Once a week, about seventy children, including those in my division, went to a small room in our activity building: Town Hall. We gathered around a very small circular black and white TV screen, watching a TV show later scorned by the black community. They believed it stereotyped their own. Division 25 was scarcely lit during this era. Turning out the lights resulted in the exact definition of total darkness. Our live-in friends saw this as an opportunity to search for crumbs. Surely twenty or so six-year-olds and a generous governess would never leave any crumbs around! While this opportunity to eat was viewed as disgusting by our governesses, we viewed this as an opportunity for a game. The game would have been difficult if not aided by the shoe repair guy.

During this era, shoes were totally leather. The only wearable parts were the soles and laces. This now unheard of design, and the cheapness of cow's hide, made it less expensive to repair shoes than buy new ones. The shoe repair shop was adjacent to Division 25. He cared deeply for the children. In a caring manner, he saved newspapers, hoping children would use them to learn to read. Hope springs eternal I guess!

Under the guise of taking those newspapers for the purpose intended, we rolled them up and stuck them in our pants. We then went over to watch that show the black community scorned. Our governess must have taken notice. However, it was probably one of those times when she really did not want to know why. After the TV show was over, we small ninjas ran back to the division, giving us lead time before our instructor arrived. With our self-made swords drawn, we lined up by the two large double doors at the entrance. We counted to three, ran into the building, and turned on the lights. Bug after bug met its demise as we wielded our weapons with expertise master ninjas would be proud to call their own. The record for kills was sixty-eight, held by the littlest thief. Not only was he the top dog cute one and a thief, and I say that lovingly, he was an exceptional swordsman. Two of us decided the record should be ours.

Steven and I were sharper than most. At least that is what we probably believed. We possessed, and I use that term in a double meaning, the capability to scheme. We noticed that the bugs always ran towards the closet. We correctly surmised that the closet was where they gained entrance, and where they had to exit. The closet was close to the back door, easy to reach before the bugs could notice us. The opportunity light bulbs lit up. We developed a strategy to give us the record. We would come in by the back door, sneak up to the closet, and stand in front of its entrance. Our ninja companions would chase the bugs toward us. We could make a killing, literally.

The day arrived to go to Town Hall. After the TV show was over, we ran back to the division, gathered at the front entrance and drew our swords. Steven and I snuck to the back entrance. After the other ninjas counted to three and turned on the light, we rushed in and stood in front of the closet door, wielding our weapons. It worked! Considerable excitement filled the air in anticipation that the record would soon be ours.

That excitement quickly changed. Our small ninja companions hastened the bug towards the closet entrance. The entrance was now a funnel for seemingly thousands of bugs. Their numbers turned into hordes, so many that they climbed over one another to make their escape. The closer they got to us, the larger they appeared to be. I could swear they had smirks on their faces, probably realizing the advantage would soon turn. They climbed over our shoes, up our legs, and some had the brass to get on our weapons. When the real war starts, I want those bugs on my side! As the bugs started gaining an upper hand, Steven's behavior changed radically. His terror was expressed with a high-pitched scream. I can only describe that scream as one you would experience from two to three thousand toddlers in an auditorium when their favorite TV personality first appears on stage. Cotton balls are highly recommended. Steven leaped onto a shelf and yelled for me to save myself. This plea was ignored. It was far more important to get the record. It did not take long to become aware that Steven's strategy was the wiser alternative. I joined him. Both of us made sounds like, "Whew, that was close."

As any builder of shelves can tell you, they are meant to hold maybe fifty pounds. You can relate to what happened if you've ever climbed out on a tree limb too far and heard a *crack*. We heard the *crack*. We glanced at each other as if one of use had some idea about what to do. Down we went. The two-by-two bins were stacked on each other, and hooked to all the shelves. Once our shelf fell, the domino effect ensured they all did. The clothes in those bins, the numerous hangers with coats, shelves with shoes, bedding, and everything else in that closet ended up on top of us. We sat there among the mess, sort of in shock. Up walked our governess. Her look resembled one Mom used to give me when I did something outrageous. Mom would sigh and tell Dad to deal with it. As handing this off to Dad was not an option, our governess had to execute another very well-known strategy. All parents exhibit thru the sound of their voices the urgency for children to do what they say. One level of urgency was interpreted as "maybe"; seldom obeyed. Another level was interpreted as, "We better do it"; somewhat obeyed. The level that demanded quick conformance was interpreted as, "We will all die a very painful death if we don't obey." You know which one the governess used finding us among all those clothes.

The next day, while the other children played, we two *smarter* children had to clean up the mess. I counted 101 dead bugs, far more than the record. The claim, however, fell on deaf ears. The other children said we had cheated. To this day, I still maintain Steven and I held the record.

NUTRITION

For a long time, it was assumed that all my homies held on to the same hope of hopes; that our parents would soon come to take us back home. While in Division 25, a new boy became part of our family. He shook that assumption. Robert kept to himself, scootering with one of the two scooters provided by a sponsor. I asked Robert if I could play with him. We raced our scooters down the walkway from our Division to the laundry nearby. During one race, Robert suddenly stopped. One of those water bugs was casually making its way across our raceway. I cannot imagine its surprise, and certainly not mine, when Robert grabbed it, popped off its head, tore off its wings, squeezed out some disgusting stuff, and threw the remains in his mouth. He took a couple of quick crunches and swallowed! My curiosity overcame my astonishment. An inquiry was made as to why Robert ate this bug. Robert explained that he had learned to eat bugs before coming to the home. In hindsight, he must have survived by eating bugs!

Robert commenced to give me some lessons on eating bugs. I never ate any, and I am sticking with that story. He warned me about spiders. You needed a lot of them to make a good meal, and some bit. It occurred to me that Robert's hope of hopes was very different than mine. While I feared that my parents would never come to get me, he probably feared they would. I realized all of us suffered differently, some very differently. While I never thought it to be disgusting to take part in that banquet of the bugs, it was somewhat advantageous knowing others would.

THE SCOOTER THIEF

A larger child had a nasty habit of taking our scooters whenever he wanted. This scooter thief was also the king of the dare and double dares, a status he held in high regard. Pride is good. Too much can be dangerous. At the innocent age of six, Robert and I devised a payback plan for taking our scooters. We knew that this king of dares would want to retain his crown. We confronted him with some dares and double dares. We lost all of them; expectedly so. During this time, the boy's peer group had gathered around, praising him for meeting the challenges. We then dared this not so innocent, but obviously unwary boy, to eat a bug. Robert and I had to go first. The boy and his peers were surely disgusted at seeing us eat a bug. However; his peers were more interested to see if their hero would meet the challenge. Don't you just love peer groups! The look on this boy's face was precious as he realized that only by eating a bug could he remain top dog of the dare and double dare. Like I said, pride can be dangerous. But his peer group was watching! He made that inevitable mistake. Even more precious was the look on his face while eating the bug, especially when he did not remove the head, wings, and the disgusting stuff! Afterwards, this boy never again saw us as easy victims when he wanted a scooter. The bug eating was also used in the very first prank played on yours truly.

GANGS

A sibling reminded me of this memory at homecoming. Division 25 was on the same side of the lake as the older boys' divisions. Occasionally, brothers of children in Division 25 came over to play with their siblings; in the true sense of the word. On one occasion, a boy's older brother took a toy away from one child and gave it to his brother. This prompted some of us to form a gang to protect against these situations. The favorite meeting place was the most beautiful fountain at the home, complements of a very dedicated greenhouse keeper.

In the center of the fountain was a statue of a mother holding her baby, or of a boy and girl, I cannot recall which. Water poured out of an umbrella they held, simulating a rain. The water landed in a circular, cement pool about twenty feet wide and three feet deep. During the summer, this fountain was surrounded by a variety of beautiful flowers and bushes, complements of an extremely dedicated person charged with maintaining the home grounds. There was no area of the home that lacked his efforts. I know because I had to water those efforts. It took me the whole day to do it. While his efforts ensured beautiful flowers and bushes surrounded this fountain, it also ensured any on the inside of the fountain was well hidden from view. The governesses loved the breathtaking beauty of this fountain. To preserve that beauty, they preached loud and often for us to stay away. Their wishes and our need for a secret meeting place were opposite companions. Ours won out and it became a favorite gathering place. Well hidden behind the surrounding flowers and bushes, we played a simple game of walking along the edge of that fountain, going faster and faster with each loop. The winner was the last to fall off, either into the pool, or safely on the outside. Gentle nudges ensured the appropriate side. We also removed our shoes and socks, rolled up our pants, sat on the outside edge of the pool, and kicked our feet in the water. I assume we participated in kid talk, whatever that was.

On one occasion, we had a serious discussion about the incident when a toy was taken away from one of us by an older boy, and given to his brother. We pledged to band together and protect our toys when older boys came over. To show commitment to the pledge, we all had to participate in a ceremony, doing something outrageous. As Robert was part of our gang, the bug eating was mentioned. Sort of wish we had known about the pinky finger promise! We agreed to eat a bug to show our commitment. Robert rounded up some fine specimens and prepared them for sacrifice. Simultaneously, we repeated the pledge, ceremoniously threw the victims into our mouths, made two quick crunches, and swallowed, just like Robert instructed. I submit that this show of allegiance is unparalleled in the annuals of commitments. While recalling this at homecoming, it was revealed that the only one who ate the bug was me! Even Robert faked eating a bug. It was the first prank played on me at the home, but certainly not the last. Regardless, I submit it had to be the best prank ever played. It does no good to play a prank unless the prankee realizes he has been pranked and who the prankers are. Those were choices of words learned from watching a popular TV show at the Town Hall activity center. I learned of this prank about twenty years later! Did those children get together all those years and laugh, knowing I still had never realized I had been pranked? I must take my hat off to them.

THE BAT GAME

We slept in old cast iron military-style beds, on those old, captive mattresses. Everyone slept in the same large dormitory on the second floor of Division 25. Above that floor was the attic, home to several hundred bats. They entered and exited via an attic window. For unknown reasons this window was left open. Perhaps one of the home staff was a bat lover. Our and the bats' homes were adjacent to the shallow end of Lake Graham, an ideal hatching ground for many bugs. Those bugs were a favorite food of the bats. The attic served as a lakeside, five-star hotel for the bats, next to a premier restaurant. We children and the bats lived in perfect harmony! During the day, we played while the bats slept. At twilight, the bats came out. They spent the night eating bugs while we slept. While we lived with bats, there were very few bugs.

While our very nice Division 25 governess seemed terrified of bats, we children ignored them. At least until one of more adventurous ones decided to go where no bat had gone before. Now, we had pillow fights at times, which our governess briefly allowed before threatening us with the voice interpreted as, "We will die a very painful death if we do not obey." order to go to sleep. As this adventurous bat flew around the dormitory, we attempted to hit it with our pillows. It was futile to hit these stealthy flyers because of their radar. But we had to try. Occasionally, the bat would take a time out, landing on the ceiling corner. It left itself vulnerable. We quit swinging. I would like to say we did this out of a sense of fairness. To be honest, we needed the rest more than the bat. The governess came out to quell what she believed was the usual pillow fight. She quickly retreated to her safe haven upon seeing the bat.

Our efforts to hit the bat became a game. Whoever gets the bat wins! We quickly made up the rules. We could not leave our beds, could not throw the pillows, and could not hit the bat while it was resting. What fun! After about an hour of this, we were all tired, but the bat was still game. The governess must have panicked and called for help. One of the home staff arrived with a tennis racket. It was fun watching him attempt to hit the bat. Alas, he was finally successful. I think many of us spent a long time crying for the bat.

A couple of the more creative children, if one can use that adjective loosely, hatched a plan to re-create this game. Who in their right mind would venture to the attic and make the retrieval? There appeared to be two kinds of bats. The smaller black bats were chosen over the larger brown ones. Their lack of size would make them much harder to hit. The unfortunate participant was retrieved and placed in a shoe box. It was pampered up to the night of the game. After saying our bedtime prayers and the governess retiring, the game was on. I can recall no instance when a bat was hit. It certainly was fun trying. When one of the home staff came over with the tennis racket we all screamed our objection to killing the bat. He went out and came back with this huge butterfly net. The victorious bat was spared and given its freedom, at least to my knowledge. This experience gave some insight into stories about gladiators.

DEAD ONES

Recently I was watching a popular TV series in which ghastly looking dead ones terrified the living, walking toward them while inviting them for dinner. I recalled a similar event that occurred in Division 25. Because we children lived, slept, ate, schooled, and played together, contagious diseases spread unchecked. When one child sneezed, the rest of us automatically went for the tissues.

One year, a pox hit very hard. I'm not sure which one. Sick children in Division 25 were quarantined to the upstairs bedroom. The well-ones played downstairs with the toys. This did not sit well with we diseased ones. A payback plan was hatched. After the well-ones left to eat, we diseased ones made our way downstairs into the room where they played with the toys. We hid behind whatever was available and waited. When the well-ones returned, we sprang up and ran towards them. We held our arms open in pretense to hug them, and smacked our lips in pretense to kiss them. The well ones were terrified of these pretenses, as our governess had often preached that they would lead to sickness. The well-ones screamed and ran, as did the governess. I cannot speak for others, but this diseased one laughed and laughed. The enforcer came and enforced the quarantine. Nowadays, as I view those movies in which the dead terrorize the undead, I keep seeing the looks of those dead ones on the faces of my diseased siblings. Likewise, I see the looks of those being terrorized on the faces of my other siblings. I would now like to apologize to all for that ill-conceived prank. (LOL)

EXPELLED

Immediately after moving to Division 25, we were informed all would be attending kindergarten. Not knowing exactly what that was, we interpreted that as interfering with our play time. However, our governess seemed excited, and we probably shared her enthusiasm. Kindergarten was a good escape from the usual division life. My kindergarten education was short.

The classroom had two very tall storage containers used to store very large blocks. These blocks were used to construct forts and other things during play time. The storage containers had tall sides, too tall for us small children to see over. Although large, the blocks were very light, fortunately for one of my siblings. The teacher assigned the job of putting the blocks away to yours truly. Someone trusted me to do something! I took this task seriously. After play time, the blocks were gathered and thrown into the storage containers. Unbeknownst to me, one of my siblings had climbed into one of the containers. He was allegedly hit several times. He cried and broke that seemingly unbroken rule. He told! The teacher and the home must have been concerned about violent children. I was unceremoniously expelled from kindergarten!

During my internment, several people in suits visited. They asked questions and showed me what seemed to be very strange pictures. I was excited to describe one group of pictures as they reminded me of my friends, the bats. While my friends were at kindergarten, I played by myself at the division. Expelled from the educational system and forced to play by myself, it proved to be very educational. It was a very ironic consequence indeed.

READING

My governess noticed I was bored. She suggested helping the shoe shop guy. His shop was upstairs, adjacent to my division. As explained before, back in those days the shoes were all made of leather. Only the soles and laces wore away. It was cheaper to replace them than buy new ones. Up the stairs to the shoe shop I went. The first job was to retrieve shoes. It was very boring. Noticing this, the shoe repair guy asked if I would like to learn to read. With boredom being the only other option, I answered in the affirmative. Is it not interesting how the punishment for a very bad act allowed me to better myself? The shoe repair guy saved newspapers with the hope that they would be used by the Division 25 children to read. Each day, I got one of these newspapers and sat by his side as he read to me, carefully pointing out the words as he read. I took to reading like the flies did to our peanut butter and jelly sandwiches. Before long, he repaired the shoes while I read the latest news, occasionally running over to have him sound out and explain a word.

PROMOTION

It was an exciting time for my friends. They were being promoted to the first grade. Not so for this violent offender. I was very sad, realizing my friends would no longer be with me. I was quietly reading a newspaper, sitting alone under the stairs leading up to the shoe shop. I heard several of the home staff nearby discussing a war. One mentioned that they were still fighting. I interrupted and informed them that the newspaper reported one side surrendered. They seemed surprised. Probably not because I knew something they did not, but because I could read. One of them asked me to read to him. We sat down on the stairs, and I read. Without saying anything, he got up and quickly walked away. Later, I was informed I would be promoted to the first grade with my friends. Is it not interesting how someone seemingly so insignificant as a shoe repair guy could make such an earth-moving change in a child's life? I never thanked him. Perhaps to some that was not necessary.

FREE POPCORN AND SISTERS

Parents surely cherish times when their children are out of their hair. It is that unique time when they can enjoy that which they surrendered when becoming parents. The more children they have, certainly the more appreciative they are of these moments. Imagine the ecstasy when a mom can send twenty to thirty of her little darlings elsewhere, leaving her to enjoy time alone. Our governess in Division 25 experienced that ecstasy once a week. Town Hall was an activity building revered by the children It surely was worshiped as a god-send by the governesses. At the age of six, we were paid about seven cents a week, enticement to do our chores. The candy store at Town Hall was the only opportunity for us to spend our income.

Children that misbehaved were issued demerits, losing some or all of what they were paid for doing chores. Losing their pay meant they had to become good friends with one that could buy candy, popcorn, and pop. Those that enjoyed the finer things in life were very good. Others made sure they had plenty of friends.

It was the day for Town Hall. Consequences of a demerit, I was a penny short to buy a bag of popcorn. An older girl working at the store must have felt sorry for me. She gave me this huge bag of popcorn – for free! She repeated this several times. Suddenly, I was the man. Other children surrounded the town hall like vultures, waiting until I came out with the popcorn.

I told one of my siblings, "I think she likes me."

His response was, "Idiot! That is your sister!"

I was shocked. I had forgotten I had sisters! The home separated siblings and had very few organized events to ensure sisters and brothers interacted on a regular basis. Without this interaction, I forgot about them. Getting free popcorn was very fortunate in remembering them.

10

Lake Graham

My story would not be complete without mentioning Lake Graham. During the inception of the home, a large valley in the center of the home grounds, and a natural spring, enabled a small lake to be created. Its initial purpose was as a water source. When other means were used to get water, it was left unattended by man. Over the many years, the environment transformed man's artificial creation into a wonderful, natural lake. There were more blue gills than can be imagined. They were easy pickings using a special bread, complement of one of our own. Two to five-pound bass kept the small fish and frogs on their toes, and as difficult it is to imagine, the cute little ducklings in the spring. The favorite fishes of fishermen could be seen nesting. They were never caught as they nested, and infrequently otherwise. Deep bass voices of bullfrogs were heard at the shallow end of the lake during the twilight. Capturing one of them would guarantee a winner of the annual frog jumping contest. Very large, scary, snapping turtles freely went their way, consequences of their size and defense mechanisms. Small turtles were not so fortunate, and just about all of us had one, the only pets allowed. They could show their stuff at the turtle Olympics. They were placed in the middle of different size circles. The first to reach the boundary of the circle was the winner. We tempted them to run out using flies, or banged on the ground. One very good side effect was to rid the division of those pesky flies.

THE BAKER

An interesting and unbelievable aspect of fishing was the blue gill's preference for a baker's bread. This baker was once a homie. He came back and was responsible for the most wonderful home-made bread and cakes, no pun intended. He must have put a secret ingredient in his bread. We moistened his bread, made a little ball of dough, attached it to a hook, and watched a scene resembling a Piranha attack. Those blue gills must have become addicted to our baker's secret ingredient. The interesting aspect of this was that other bread dough from outside the home did not bring that response. It was very funny to watch outsiders come with their own bread dough. While they rarely caught a fish, us homies right next to them raked them in.

"SWIMMING" IN LAKE GRAHAM

Swimming in Lake Graham was an activity that almost every homie enjoyed. I cannot speak for the girls, but we boys saw fit to act our stupidest during swimming. Maybe it was because the lake was well in sight of the girls' divisions, or perhaps because we were just stupid. Whatever the reason, *swimming* in Lake Graham was without a doubt the favorite activity in the summer. Mooning was one of the favorite antics in the 50s. Our enforcer sternly warned us about doing that, as the swimming hole was well in sight of the girl's divisions. We could not help to notice the smile on his face while he warned us. Seeing who could be the most ridiculous jumping off the diving board was one of our favorite competitions. There were some that took this diving seriously. I could not help to notice the stark difference in their efforts and ours.

Many of us took advantage of the location of the swimming hole at the lake. It was well in sight of the girls. The more serious ones took advantage of this with a very specific objective, quite different than that we stupid ones held dearly. They wanted to showcase themselves to the ladies. I hate to say I laughed at my homies, but I treasured the moments when those egos sought to impress the ladies. One moment was especially precious.

We lined up to take turns jumping off the diving board. We stupid ones did whatever. Our egotistic Hollywood stars had a routine that I still enjoy recalling after all these years. All of them wore very tight jock-type bathing suits, not the baggy types we stupid ones wore. These egos stood at the back of the diving board waiting their turn. They took this opportunity to adjust their bathing suits just low enough to be legal, if you know what I mean. They then adjusted their hair. I tell no lie when I say that one of them carried a comb inside his bathing suit! When their turn came, they waited patiently for the previous diver to get out of the water, making sure they were the only possible focus of their audience. They then very methodically stepped on the diving board and glanced up ever so slightly, to make sure they their admirers were looking. When they took too long, I had to engage in a song popular from a 50s movie, starting with lyrics describing one as so pretty. Needless to say, I was not appreciated by these egotistic stars. Once convinced the ladies were paying attention, they posed, as if their admirers could take pictures. They stood straight up, shoulders back, with their arms by their sides. They shook their heads, as if to convince those watching it took a brave man indeed to try the dive they were about to attempt. Very methodically they strutted out to the end of the board, bounced twice, and like Olympic divers performed their usual, wonderful, swan-like dives. Although a distance away, one could hear the sighs from the girls. Our responses of course were somewhat different. These pretty ones then surfaced, always right near the steps leading out of the water. They got out of the lake, turned towards the girls and appeared to bow, in appreciation of their sighs. They then arranged their hair, their bathing suit, turned around, seemingly to showcase their posterior, then strutted like a peacock back towards the back of the diving board. I cannot speak for the others, especially the girls, but I swear to God I laughed myself silly at this spectacle. I made it a point to take my turn right after one of these pretty ones. I entertained the girls with something much different. The girls were always invited to watch the annual diving competition. I never missed a single one. The show for me was very entertaining, much different than what the girls enjoyed, if you know what I mean.

For the rest of us that liked to act stupid, those funny three comics extremely popular in this era, and that group of cops popular in another era, could not match our antics. That the lake provided the best of good times can be verified from the bucket lists of many of us homies. Looking out over Lake Graham during homecoming, there is an urge to jump in one last time. I think I felt a tear making its way down my cheek every time I left Homecoming without doing this.

11

Preteen Years

ach year the children were moved into another division. We in Division 25 were sent to Divisions 8 and 9. I must admit, the best times at the home was when I was in Division 9.

FRED

Behind those divisions was a steep bank leading down to the shallow end of Lake Graham. While our governesses preached loud and often about avoiding that lake, it was an irresistible temptation. The only real danger was getting stuck in about two feet of mud. Many ended up there. Not by my hand. (LOL) Favorite activities at the shallow part of the lake were turtling and frogging in the two feet of mud. The latter was the best option, as the former were the snapping kind. The deep base voices of these billion-year-old species pleading to the ladies gave away their locations. Once under water and the mud, they were safe. One unfortunate bullfrog must have been asleep. Kevin easily caught it. We named it Fred. Fred was treated like a celebrity. He received free rent in a five-star hotel with daily banquets of fresh food, water, flies, and greens. Fred proved to be a very unusual frog. He never moved, not ever. Despite our attempts to get him to jump, he simply sat still, seemingly unaware of what he was supposed to do.

One day, Fred decided to stretch his legs. The results were sensational. Never had I seen, or certainly never will see, leaps the distance of Fred's. We entered him into the annual frog jumping festival. We arrived with Fred near the back of Morton Memorial High School, where the festival was held. After watching the other frogs warm up, we realized that Fred was, hands down, the better leaper. Fred was about to achieve immortality. I opened the shoe box to allow Fred to get more oxygen, preparing him for his time in the sun. I then turned around to watch the contest.

A couple of minutes later Kevin look down at Fred's hotel and asked, "Where is Fred?"

We looked down the walkway next to the school. There was Fred, making tremendous leaps, heading towards the valley at the front of the school. We chased him, but he easily made it. I could swear that on his final leap, he turned around in midair and gave us a salute, as if to say, "See ya later suckers."

Fred was well camouflaged in the deep grass of the valley. We never found him. We were extremely disappointed that a sure thing was not to be had. We never again caught a frog like Fred. Even if we had, it could not possibly have matched Fred's leaps. What a frog! When retiring for the night, I often think of Fred. After all, here was a frog that could have been a superstar, a champion among champions, guaranteed a lifetime of luxury, food, and fame. All he wanted was that which we all desire: freedom.

Fred was far wiser than one could imagine in his endeavors to be free. First, Fred sat perfectly still, concealing his ability to traverse large distances quickly in a single bound, linking him to a popular super hero, which he surely was. Second, he used his instincts to gain an image of how far the valley was from where the contest was being held. Third, he initiated his escape exactly at that moment we would least expect it. Last, he had precise timing of how far he could get before we could catch him.

He carried out his escape flawlessly. Fred gave some insight into those movies where POWs plan their escapes. When I go back to homecoming, I look out over Lake Graham and give Fred a salute. What a frog!

EXTREME BASEBALL?

While watching TV, I came upon a new sport. It was referred to as X sports. I recalled a sport at the home which may be the first X sport of all time. A Division next to us held boys of the same color, and all ages. This will be explained later in this story.

Division 8, 9, 10 and 11 shared the same play area. This playground was next to a hill leading down to Lake Graham. Oftentimes, a baseball was seen rolling towards the hill leading down to the two feet of mud in the lake. The Division 11 older boys would frantically yell at us to stop it from going down that hill. We learned not to stop that ball for selfish reasons. When the ball did end up in the mud, one of the Division 11 boys had to step into that disgusting mud and retrieve that ball. We gathered at the top of the hill leading down to the lake to watch this spectacle. It was funny, in a sadistic sort of way. The source of that ball was a game that only the Division 11 boys played.

The large playground had about eight swings, four teeter totters, one or two slides, a small baseball diamond, and many other playground equipment. The Division 11 boys turned a small dirt patch behind their division into a small baseball infield. The outfield consisted of the rest of the playground, with all the playground equipment. This included the hill leading down to Lake Graham, and as far as I know, the lake itself. We smaller children did not care to play baseball with the Division 11 boys. Most were much older, and they played real baseball; i.e., with a hard ball! Our governess thought the Division 11 boys purposely excluded us and complained. After hearing the complaint, the Division 11 boys gave me a mitt and asked me to stand in right field, next to the swings. This certainly was to pacify our governess.

On the first at bat, the ball was hit to left field. The fielder ran back, hurdled the iron bar, fell over the teeter totters, got back up, dodged the slide and several other pieces of playground equipment, ran down the hill leading to the lake, and made the catch. Wow, extreme baseball!

I said to myself "Hey, this could be fun"!

The next batter hit the ball to right field, my domain. The Division II boys screamed, "Catch it, catch it."

I circled the ball, and was introduced into one of the reasons it was an X sport. I ran into the light post. I could hear the Division II boys yelling, "Get up, get up."

In keeping with the spirit of the game, I got back up and ran to make the catch. Unfortunately, I was then made well aware of why this was an extreme sport. Another child had decided to enjoy the swings, also part of right field. The collision I can still feel to this day. The Division II boys ran over and pleaded for me not to tell the governesses what had happened, as that would be the end of their extreme baseball. I was sort of insulted. We children never told, never! For the rest of the game, I stood out in right field, nursing my wounds. When the ball was hit to right field, I waited for the ball to drop before retrieving it, making sure to avoid the playground equipment. I had a lot of respect for Division II boys after that. Their form of baseball was way before its time, extreme! That was my first formal attempt at playing a real sport. It was a very painful lesson. The next sport would prove to make that pain seem like a love tap.

THE FOOTBALL GAME

There were several traditions at the home. Most were the usual ones, such as the prom, the Halloween hay ride, and so on. Some were unique to home life, created by the children themselves. The most popular of these for the boys was the annual mud football game.

Behind the East side divisions was a naturally muddy field. The same spring that fed the lake, the winter thaw, and the children, all conspired to make sure it was one bog of mud. Seniors and underclassmen put on disposable clothes, and proceeded to play against each other in a game of mud football. It was a game filled with funny antics, and little respect for the rules of real football. The game also had little respect for those skills in playing real football. Running was mostly done in place, compliments of the mud. Throwing a football covered with mud could easily make the funny highlights, and the same would be true for catching. No one wanted, or even had to, tackle another, least they find themselves sliding in the mud. Most children grabbed a handful of mud before a play, certainly to leave a little present for the opponents. No one kept score, but everyone argued about what is was, not seriously of course. Mud football was a tradition most enjoyable for all. It was especially entertaining to we small children.

Sometimes, the participants would get the younger ones into the act. On one occasion, a senior grabbed a child, with the governess's permission of course.

With the child in hand, and the football, he ran for the goal line, yelling, "I have a child. I have a child. Don't hurt the kid, don't hurt the kid."

The others, including his teammates, separated him from the ball and the child, disposing of him in the mud. They then rolled the child in the mud, making sure he was muddied as much as possible. In another instance, it was decided to use another child for a trick play. The smallest child in our division would be the quarterback, take the hike from under the legs of the center, and then run under the legs of the center. Of all places to expect a runner to go, it most certainly would not be from under the legs of the center! Good intentions sometimes can have the worse of outcomes. I would now like to apologize to the poor doomed center who was involved in that ill-conceived plan.

MISHAWAKA FOOTBALL

During this era, our football teams were exceptional. Considering that our school was about one fifth that of other schools, they were more than exceptional. Our fondness for mud football, and attempts to continue the tradition of being exceptional, gave us Division 8 and 9 children incentive to play football. We had no idea how to play. With the simplicity of children, we invented a game: Mishawaka Football.

Mishawaka Football was extremely popular, and certainly the most simplistic. One of us tossed the ball into the air, and everyone tackled the unfortunate that caught it. Because of my size, I chose always to be the tackler, never the "tacklee"; choices taught to us from our favorite TV show. I know of no child that refused to play this game.

As we were enjoying our game, a couple of the older boys from other divisions had some choice adjectives about our version of football. Some of my siblings had a nasty habit of facing up to that charging rhino. They responded appropriately, at least as far as they were concerned. During the confusion of yelling back and forth, out of nowhere someone yelled that the older boys were afraid to play football against us. There was dead silence, especially among us that valued our health. "Did he just challenge the older boys?" The older boys quickly accepted. We thought it would be mud football, a very fun game. To our dismay, we were informed it would be real football, a very serious game with rules and stuff.

REAL FOOTBALL?
Mud football was easy to play. It had few rules and no organization. Real football had both these characteristics. We knew nothing about each. One of us held our health above all other concerns, and sought reasons to protect the same. To this end, I questioned the wisdom of challenging others to play a game we knew nothing about, especially with much bigger children. However, my friends had the nasty habit of not backing down from challenges. Most looked forward to the day any were offered. Unfortunately, I had the nasty habit of being loyal.

During our first practice session, our governess realized we had no idea how to play. She volunteered to teach us. Unfortunately, her knowledge was just a smidge above ours. After about a week of practice, we still had no idea how to play. But we had to meet the challenge! One of the older Division II boys came over to watch us. After some time, he inquired as to what we were doing. Apparently, we were so bad it was not obvious! When we told him about the challenge, he felt sorry for us and volunteered to be the coach! We all cheered. The loudest cheer came from our governess.

LOOK BEFORE YOU LEAP!

This challenge was interesting. It was the understanding that the south side divisions would play against the east side divisions. The boys in the south side divisions were all older, and I might add, bigger. However, the south side division boys must have forgot that there was one division which did have older boys. The Division 11 boys were of all ages. We younger ones were excited, realizing they could play. Two of the Division 11 boys were extremely talented. One would average sixteen yards every time he touched the football in high school. Both were college stars, and one became a very popular NFL star. The Division 11 brothers who became stars could play with us! Our adversaries quickly saw the writing on the wall and complained that Division 11 boys were not included in the challenge. Realizing it was unfair, we younger children followed our hearts instead of our logic. We agreed that the Division 11 boys were not included. We did insist they could be coaches. Congrats to us for recognizing fairness. Shame on us for stupidity.

PRACTICE MAKES PERFECT

On the first day of practice, we gave additional significance to the *try* in try-outs. No one could throw the ball, which was of no consequence, as no one could catch it. Kicking was out of the question, as it hurt too much. Our perception of a quarterback seemed to be that he got the ball first. I believe that John, our coach, aged a bit during his coaching tenure. Two children larger than most of us had this amazing characteristic of carefully weighing the consequences of just about all they were about to experience. They then discarded all that made no sense. I called them the no-nonsense kids. Realizing the nonsense of playing against the bigger kids, we did not expect them to volunteer. We sighed a sense of relief when loyalty won the day. More encouragement came when our biggest sibling also volunteered. Carroll was one no child wanted to find out what punishment awaited if he was wronged. It was difficult to distinguish Carroll's running from walking. He grew so fast that he was absent of any coordination to speak of. Later we would be chasing the baseballs he hit, so far he could easily walk around the bases. Regardless, he was a very tender child, eager to be part of our family.

Noticing that the linemen seemed to bash against each other, I did not volunteer for that position. This should have been one of the smartest decisions in my life. However, one of my best friends quickly volunteered. He had an altercation with an older boy earlier that year. The license to bash that older boy was just too tempting. My sense of loyalty took over. I also volunteered to be a lineman. To any small child reading this, avoid volunteering simply from a sense of loyalty. The consequences can be painful. After a few days of practicing, it was obvious we were overmatched, but we had to meet the challenge.

THE BIG GAME

On the day of the game, there was standing room only. Literally, there was standing room only as there were no seats. Actually, there were no discernible boundary makers, no yardage lines, no touchdown markers, and no goal posts. The field was what one could refer to as a virtual football field.

We did a lot of, "It looks like ten yards.", "Close enough.", "I was not out of bounds.", "You were out of bounds.", and many other phrases intermingled with expletives. Any time one got close to the goal line or ran out of bounds, those who yelled the loudest usually got their way. The bigger boys usually won those arguments. All the boys' divisions and home staff were in attendance.

We lost the coin toss, if you want to interpret *lost* literally. We *kicked off*, a term to us that meant to throw the ball to the other team. We quickly learned hurt would not be in short supply. Some of my tougher colleagues seemed excited about the action, getting knocked down, yelling something unintelligible, getting back up, and doing it all over again. Others were not too enthusiastic about repeating that scenario but loyal to the cause.

Many of us were somewhat in that zone of "I have to do this or else my friends will disown me. Please God, don't let me get hurt."

On the first series of downs, I had a vision that illustrates what we faced. Remember movies in which the Roman legions formed a square group, placed their shields on all sides and above their heads, and then proceeded to march undeterred through the enemy? This vision was not far removed from reality. That we got our butts kicked at the beginning would be a huge understatement. The other team scored after a set of very, very short offensive plays. They kicked off to us, which is literally what happened. Tom, our best athlete, caught the ball. Every Halloween I seem to recall his fate. However, a martyr he became, and his demise made the rest of us more determined. The two no-nonsense kids, along with others, decided enough was enough. They stopped the older boys in their tracks. John proved to be a very good coach. Despite the setbacks, he continued to encourage us We finally were convinced we could win. In turn, we started encouraging each other to try harder. Finally, the tide turned our way.

Larry was an excellent quarterback, but he quickly met the same fate as Tom. After he was forced to retire, John asked for volunteers to take over that position. Normally, one would be excited about being selected for such an important position. However, my take was that proximity to the ball was not necessarily a good thing. Instrumental in my decision to volunteer was the realization that although the quarterback got the ball first, he also decided who got the ball last. After some time of implementing this strategy, my *friends* decided to teach me a lesson. On the next play, they hit the ground, leaving me all alone with the ball and those it seemed to attract. After that painful lesson, I took my turns, or at least enough that the others thought I was.

Handing off the ball proved to be a challenge, as one of the more athletic boys on the opposite team spent most of his time in our backfield. Dodging him just to hand off the ball was a problem. Although Tom had been retired earlier, he was a trooper and re-entered the game as a running back. He was destined to be a track star and extremely efficient in avoiding others, a talent most beneficial in dealing with that kid who liked our backfield. With Tom's efforts, those of the two no-nonsense kids, and the support from the rest of us, we scored several times!

Near the end of the game we were desperate to score. An amazing series of events transpired. Either John decided to give Carroll a chance, or Carroll simply decided enough was enough. No one would dare argue with him about that. We tried to offer him advice on what to do. He laughed, ignored us, and stood next to the line of scrimmage. When the opponents handed the ball off, the runner ran right towards Carroll, surely thinking it would be easy to dodge someone with little or no coordination. The lineman opposite Carroll quickly found himself on his butt, as did the blockers for the runner. Carroll grabbed the runner, pulled him over, and appeared to convince him to give up the ball. Carroll then promptly walked towards the goal. When I say walk, I mean walk. Carroll grew so fast you could not distinguish between his running and walking. The fifth and sixth graders jumped on him, making Carroll the equivalent of the bus transportation system. Some of us others realized what was happening, ran over, and started physically removing kids from Carroll. For the rest of the game, we started kicking butts, but we were too far behind, and alas we lost.

After the game, John got us together and told us we should be proud. We let out what best can be described as a whispered yell and dragged our butts back to our divisions, black and blue. I could not help but notice the older kids did the same. The older boys never again questioned us about our games. We younger children were proud of our effort. For myself, I made it a point to think long and hard before making challenges.

HORSE

The state must have included the requirement "Must be wonderful." on the job applications. At the expense of seeming shallow, our first governess in Division 9 not only was that, she was very young and very pretty. There were many impressionable young boys who would support me on that characterization. Her tenure at the home was very short, which I attributed to the horse.

Remember the promise that there would be horses? Well, there was at least one, and it was a very big horse. A brick-lined road wound itself behind the boys' divisions. Every morning, right after sunrise, clickty-click sounds of a horse's hoofs against those bricks woke us. This musical alarm silenced momentarily, then continued, becoming louder the closer it got to our division. This wake-up alarm was courtesy of a horse pulling a wagon used to collect stuff accumulated daily in the divisions. True to the simplicity of young children, we named the horse, "Horse."

When we first encountered this beast of burden, it was obvious hygiene was not a priority. Horse's mane and fur were dull, with large clumps of hair mingled with dirt. A brush, comb, and scissors borrowed from our pretty, young governess's bathroom changed that. After a few weeks, Horse's mane and hair were clean, smooth, and shiny like a new penny. Horse's diet also improved considerably. During meals, we stuffed carrots, apples, lettuce, and other food items into our shirts. Though against the ivory tower rules, they were not against those rules the governesses enforced. Horse very quickly became the horse about town, and I do not say that because Horse was the only horse in town. While Horse was the focus of our efforts, some events unraveled that made us believe our pretty, young governess was the focus of the young man driving the wagon.

LOVE IS IN THE AIR?

While we groomed and fed Horse, the young man driving the wagon temporarily disappeared. He appeared later, sometimes much later. With a quick smile and a clicking sound, away went Horse, the wagon, stuff, and the young man. This went on for several months. Suddenly, our young, pretty governess and this young man left the home, at about the same time. Let's recapitulate. The horse would stop behind our division, right next to the porch railing. Most conveniently, that railing was just a step away from the roof. Even more conveniently, the window of the room where our very pretty, young governess slept was just a few steps away. While we fed Horse, the young man disappeared, magically appearing sometime later. Later in the year, the young man and our very young, very nice, and very pretty governess left the home, precisely at the same time. I always wondered whether love made its presence known for that young man and our lovely young governess?

RUN HORSE RUN

Horse continued to visit, only with a much older man. He never temporarily disappeared like the other. This gave us little time to feed and groom Horse. One morning, the musical hoofs were replaced by the sound of a tractor. The tractor was super cool but could not be groomed and fed. We asked what happened to Horse. We were told that Horse had been put out to pasture. We interpreted that literally. The older boys let us know that meant the glue factory. Billie and I were devastated. We had to make sure Horse was okay.

The next morning, we followed the tractor and wagon as it made its rounds around a very long, winding road behind the boys' divisions. We ended up next to a huge barn. We entered the barn, walked between stalls too high to see over, and called out for Horse. We eventually ended up at the end of the barn, where there were large stalls with iron bars. In one stall was Horse. Horse's head hung so low it almost touched the ground, a far cry from the majestic appearance of which we were familiar. Horse's mane was dull, with clumps of hair. Its fur was crusted with dirt and other stuff too nasty to believe. Its stall was filled with hay and crap, so much that it would be impossible to lie down without being soiled. Horse used every bit of strength just to raise his head, as if to thank us for visiting. We showed Horse some carrots we had borrowed from the kitchen. Horse slowly approached and ate a few. He showed little enthusiasm about eating.

After words of encouragement, we said goodbye and made our way back towards the barn doors. Halfway out of the barn, Billie broke down. He yelled that we had to free Horse. We ran back to Horse's stall. The stall had a huge lock on it, much like one would see on prison doors in those old movies. The keys were hanging on hooks right next to the stalls. Horse immediately became alert when we opened its stall. Horse hastily made its way out of the stall and went towards the barn doors.

Once again, we heard those familiar clickty-click sounds of hoofs; now an octave lower as they were on cement. Upon reaching the doors, Horse turned its head towards us, as if to ask us to open the door, which we did. Horse immediately surveyed the area, trotted over to some very tall grass by the roadway, and munched away. We tried to convince Horse to run, to avoid the glue factory. Horse would get a clump of grass, look at us, and continue to munch away. Perhaps Horse knew its fate and simply wanted a last supper. Billie and I finally guided Horse to the back of the barn, out of danger of the highway, and left. We convinced ourselves that the horse eventually found its freedom. I can still hear in my mind those clickty-clock sounds of its hoofs hitting that brick-paved roadway. We loved that horse! While we had lost our young, pretty governess, and a horse we loved, we gained who I believe was the best governess at the home.

DEATH

Our new governess sympathized with us about our young, pretty governess leaving. Over time, we came to adore her as much, if not more. Events unfolded that would have everlasting effects on many of us.

We gathered around our governess right before bedtime as she read stories. During the middle of a story, she suddenly clutched her heart. With a tortured voice, she ordered us to bed. She instructed two of the children to stay with her. Later she started screaming.

The words I can still hear. "Oh God, not now, please not now. Billy, don't let this happen to you. Don't let this happen to you."

We were terrified. It was obvious our wonderful governess was suffering enormous pain. We yelled for Billy to get someone to help her. Some tried in vain to use the telephone. Billy started to leave several times to get help.

He stopped when our governess yelled "Billy, don't leave me. Please don't leave me."

I cannot recall how help was obtained, but eventually, an ambulance arrived. Our wonderful governess became quieter, a huge relief to us who loved her. Relief changed to the worst of fears when our wonderful governess became completely silent. As she was carried away, we asked one of the home staff if she would be okay. Forcing himself not to cry, he told us to get some sleep. We insisted on an answer.

He turned towards us, obviously having difficulty speaking. He finally said, "She has gone to heaven."

Death's presence was extremely traumatizing. The home staff must have recognized this. They arranged to have a priest visit. His explanations gave me the impression that God had summoned our governess to heaven. I could not understand why God had chosen this wonderful angel. I understood less why he had taken her with so much suffering. This experience would influence my spiritual being and affect a perfect attendance at church.

CHURCH

The most beautiful structure in Indiana resides on the grounds of the former Indiana Soldiers and Sailors Children's Home. Lincoln Hall is an old Civil War theatre. On Sundays, it was used for church services. Church was an integral part of life at the home. Attendance was mandatory and Christianity the only religion. My attendance at church was affected by my eight-year old reasoning about the death of our governess. My reasoning was I could not be summed away if God did not know I existed. To that end, I skipped the church services, as I was taught that was God's house. I was never discovered as missing. Apparently, a headcount was never conducted during church services, or the governesses never cared if anyone skipped.

Before church services started, children could use the bathrooms, located in the basement at the back of this old Civil War theatre. The proximity of the basement to the back doors of the church, offered an irresistible temptation to skip church. Home staff were aware of this. One guarded these exits before the church services started. When services were to start, they emptied out the bathrooms, sending the children into the church proper. Thereafter, one of the home staff kept track of who went and came back from the bathroom. It was the perfect plan to ensure all stayed at church. However; the fallacies of mankind extend to that which they create. Children's ingenuities were not challenged in overcoming this deterrent. A hole in the basement wall was the fallacy. This hole was created to allow convenient access to the utility tunnels. One only had to fake a bathroom visit before services started, go down into the basement and crawl into that hole, out of sight. Once home staff cleared out the children from the basement, escape was made through the utility tunnel. One had to crawl from the hole, beneath the stage to get to the utility tunnel. The escape was postponed temporarily. Unlike other churches, the school choir was also the church choir, making church both a religious and entertaining experience. I never missed a performance, although listening to them below the stage where they sang was somewhat different than in the church proper. The utility tunnel led to the school. This initially created a problem. The tunnel's entrance at the school was locked from the outside of the tunnel. The lock was well in sight of the janitors. Removing it was not an option. One of my friends came up with the ingenious idea of removing the door latches each Friday. Evidently everyone focused on the lock, and took little notice of the latches. A push on the door inside the tunnel detached the door. After escaping from the tunnel, these door latches were put back in place. Such a simple idea.

Church time was spent at the school or talking to the animals in a barn across the highway next to the church. On more than one occasion, teachers and farm workers were encountered. On more than one occasion, the same ones. They also adhered to that unbroken rule. They never told, never! We simply waved to each other and went our own ways. I found that one could wander throughout the entire home while church services were conducted! No one worked on Sunday, no one cared about church skippers, and all the others were in Church. When the other children were noticed leaving church, I made my way back to the division. I looked forward to *attending* church. The governesses must have mistaken this as a fondness for church. I was selected as one of several to be awarded a medal for perfect church attendance over several years. The medals were to be awarded during a church service. I was unaware of this. In what has to be true justice, I could not accept the medal. I was not there! I would have accepted the medal. After all, I had attended church. My attempt to hide from God would cause me to go down a path that would affect my spiritual life. A reminder of just how was assisted by the night watchman at the home.

MY SPIRITUAL SELF

While working at the home during the summer, I stayed in an apartment on the home grounds. Being a night owl, the night watchman and I became friends. He shared some interesting midnight moments that the home staff would not appreciate anyone writing about. My lips will forever be sealed about those. He also shared some midnight moments of we children. Our lips have never been sealed about those. He mentioned a file kept in an unusual place, right below the countertop where the home signed in visitors. He told me it was labeled with my name and another's who he believed was a priest from a nearby town. He left to go on his rounds. I did what any American boy would do. The file contained a narrative about religions, one that I had written during my senior year at the home, only one year earlier. Reading that narrative reminded me of how our governess's death affected my spiritual self.

The struggle with the death of our wonderful governess, and the painful way she was summoned, caused me to wonder if other religions handled death differently. This dominated my thoughts for several years. I decided to investigate other religions. Over the next few years, I practiced several, each for several months. From this experience, I concluded that it matters little which religion they practice, as long as they preach goodness and respect for others.

For my senior English class, I wrote a paper describing the differences and similarities between religions, along with the conclusion above. This paper was in the file eluded to by the night watchman. Evidently, the English teacher thought this conclusion was inappropriate. He shared his concern with the superintendent of the home. The superintendent must have agreed with the teacher. He arranged for a priest to pay me a visit.

This priest and I went to the back room of Division 27. For the better part of the afternoon I stuck to my conclusion, and he explained that there was only one God, and Christianity the only true religion. Finally, he said that he would pray for me and left. After that argument, my governess, who seemingly never had a good opinion about me, congratulated me for standing my ground.

This conclusion altered my spiritual self. I now believe it matter little what religion one adheres to, as long as it promotes goodness and respect. I believe God is a concept, and does not favor any one religion. I believe that it is impossible for us to completely understand God. We can study the universe and our world to understand what God has created, and possibly what is in store for us. I also believe that the concept of God has made it possible for every species to behave as they will. They, and not God, are the deciders of their fates. I also believe that heaven and hell do not exist as life after death. They exist here on Earth. We create our own heaven from the goodness we promote. We create our own hell. I have discussed this with some priests. They debunked it as rubberish. I understand that. I also believe that there is no set of beliefs, no group of persons, or philosophies, that represent the absolute truths. We all have the free will gave to us by God. When others tell me what I believe is rubberish, I understand that are talking from their perspective of truths. It surely may be rubberish to them. To me it is not.

A VERY KIND CHILD
This memory spanned the years from six to ten years of age. It is about a very unusual, and very kind, child. One lesson learned was from a very kind child. It was probably the most important lesson I took from the home.

At the age of about seven or eight, three children discovered they had common interests. They shared these together, almost always without the company of others. As a group, they seemed to exhibit a very different behavior than they did when they interacted with the rest of us. One such behavior was the considerable attention given to a new arrival at the home. This new child was a sweet child. He very much wanted to be part of our family. He would do about anything to participate with us in our games, even playing the part of an Indian in our cowboys and Indians games. In hindsight, it might have been an attempt to gain approval of the others. He was a very kind child.

Almost immediately after this kind child joined us, I noticed the three children making a point to be alone with this kind child. This attention to the kind child lasted for several months. This kind child started sleeping a lot, just about the entire afternoon. It was very strange. Sleeping was just about the last thought any of us had, especially when it was play time. I wondered if his need to sleep had something to do with all the attention he was getting from this group of three.

I and this kind child shared a love for swinging on a playground apparatus referred to as a Monkey Shine. I was waiting for him to wake up and play with me. Our governess came running out of our living quarters. She was very angry. She grabbed me by an ear, forced me inside, and locked me in the closet. All this time she asked me why I had tried to hang this kind child. I cannot accurately describe my response. I think I must have relegated it into my subconscious. It must have been traumatizing. The only *hanging* which I knew was from those old westerns. Why I was accused of such a deed was upsetting, to say the least. After several hours being locked in the closet, some suits came by. They asked me a lot of questions. After a couple of hours, they told me never to tell anyone what they had discussed. They let me go out to play. To say this experience scared me would be an understatement. I was concerned about this kind child. Did he try to hang himself?? This kind child disappeared for a few days. When he returned, I noticed a considerable change. Previously he wanted very much to participate in our games. Now he kept by himself. Not only did he keep by himself, it appeared that he was quite satisfied in doing so.

I kept my distance. I had no idea how to interact with someone who apparently tried to hang himself. Several days later I was wakened by a commotion in the back of our Division. I went to investigate. This kind child had one of his hands around one of the three children's neck, holding him against the wall.

He yelled over and over "Leave me alone"!

He tossed this unkind child aside like a rag doll and turned his attention to the two other children. They were huddled together in the corner, obviously very afraid. This kind child repeated his message to them. They tripped over themselves trying to escape. I asked this kind child if he was okay.

He responded, "Mind you own business."

For the rest of our time in that Division, and all other Divisions, these three children never exhibited the strange behavior as before. They and the kind child went their own ways. For the next few years, I could not get out of my mind exactly what happened between these three children and the kind child.

I asked myself; "Is there a connection between the behavior of the three children, the kind child sleeping all day, and an alleged attempt at a hanging"? I could never answer that question without some doubt, but there was an incident that indicated perhaps there was a connection.

When we children were initially brought together, there was little kinship. We were just children, much like children from next door. Over the years we were together, we developed very strong kinships, much like that of brothers. How you treat another you barely know is very much different than after you get to know him as your brother. I believe this played itself out with these three children and the kind child. When they first met, these three children seemed to treat this kind child much different than after they lived with him for several years. They went to great lengths to be nice to this kind child. On hindsight, I believe they may have been ashamed of how they previously treated one who now they consider their brother. I say this because of an extraordinary event that happened when we were about thirteen years old.

On our birthdays, we ate dinner quickly, then sang Happy Birthday even quicker. Waiting was a cake made by one of our own homies, a baker. It was the birthday for this kind child. We all rushed to get a piece; except for these three children. They all sat in the corner of the dining hall, talking among themselves. Not one to refuse an opportunity, I went over to one of the three children and asked if I could have his piece of cake.

He responded that he did not care. I went back to the cake-cutting table and informed the cake-cutting child, the kind child, that one of these three children sitting by themselves said I could have his piece of cake. This kind child stared at these children. Finally, he cut three pieces of cake, stuck a fork in them, took them over to the children, and gave each of them a piece of cake. He came back to cake-cutting. Curiosity got the best of me. Why did these three children refuse to get a piece of cake, and why did this kind child make sure they got a piece? Two of the three children dove in to enjoy their cakes. The other stared at his piece of cake for quite a while. He got up, turned his chair around to face a window, sat down and placed his hands in a praying position onto the window sill. He placed his head upon his hands, and cried. Our governess went over to see what was wrong. This child quickly let her know he needed no help. After witnessing this for a while, the cake-cutter went over to the child crying. He placed an arm around his shoulder, bent over and for about two to three minutes whispered something in his ear. The kind child then raised up, patted the crying child on the back, and went back to the cake-cutting. After a few minutes this crying child raised his head. He turned his chair around to the table and started eating the cake. I noticed a huge difference in his demeanor. On hindsight, I believe a huge load had been lifted off his shoulders. This child took the piece of cake over to the cake-cutting table. He told everyone they should sing happy birthday again. We all sang it again. With all that cake in our mouth; it was a very muffled birthday song.

These three children and the kind child all lived with me, or right next door to me, for the remainder of our stay at the home. More important, they lived with each other, or next door to each other. It is quite impossible for children not to develop a close kinship when they live like siblings. We all felt very close. No one mentioned that strange behavior I had noticed at our very young ages. Perhaps these memories were best forgotten. If it were not for the accusation of hanging another, this memory probably would have remained in my subconscious. I and these children all graduated from the home and went our own ways. Many, many years later, and over several years, the three children that had shared so much together passed away. Any passing is sad, but they were my brothers. It was very sad. These three children all became very successful in their endeavors after leaving the home. They all were happily married, and had what surely were wonderful children. I was very happy for them. Some years later, I got a call from one of my homies. The kind child had also left our world. I read his obituary. Like the others, he was very successful in his life. Like the others, he also married, and had what surely were very wonderful children. Knowing he had probably went thru, and endured, some very serious suffering, I cried. All the time at the home, I wanted to go over to this kind child, wrap my arms around him, and give him a big hug. Now I realize that I probably needed that hug more than he did.

12

Separate And Equal

At about the age of eight to ten years old, I lived in Divisions 9, next to Division 10 and 11. Division 10 held girls of all ages, and the same color. Division 11 held boys of all ages, and the same color as the girls next to them. We were told to refer to them as *colored people*, as strange as that may sound nowadays. On several days, the boys and girls could comingle at the most cherished structure at the home, Town Hall. I could not help to notice that two sisters from Division 10, in the true sense of the word, always played together adjacent to Town Hall, rather than comingle with the other girls inside Town Hall. This seemed odd. I inquired why they did not. They appeared uninterested in answering. Being an annoying child, I pressed for an answer.

The older sister finally held out her arm and said, "This is why."

I certainly recognized she was a different color, but I had no idea why that prevented them from going inside. My ignorance being obvious, she tried again. She explained that the reason they could not go inside was because her relatives were from Africa. That was even more confusing. I decided to drop the subject. As I still had a concern that they had to play by themselves, I told them I would play with them. The older girl smiled and told me that I should leave them alone. I was very disappointed. One should realize that in the early 50s, Indiana was not without bigotry. Surely the segregation at the home was the result of those attitudes.

SHAME, SHAME, SHAME

The Division 10 and 11 children were all the same color and all ages. This did not go unnoticed by we children. We interpreted this difference exactly for what it was; no more. More noticeable was their living arrangements. Brothers lived with brothers, and sisters with sisters. Additionally, brothers and sisters lived right next to each other. Most of us had brothers and sisters. We could not live with our brothers, and our sisters were not allowed to live right next to us. The living arrangements for the Division 10 and 11 children were viewed by many of us as preferential treatment. My frustration with this preferential treatment grew the more I thought about my sisters.

Finally, I broke down. I told the governess I was going to let the Division 10 and 11 children know how unfair it was that they got to live with their brothers and sisters. Despite her warnings to not do that, I marched over to the Division where the *colored girls* lived. I let myself in, ready to voice my frustration. Their governess stopped me and asked why I was there. I chickened out about voicing my frustration. I told a little white lie to gain entrance. I asked her if one of the girls could get a message to my sister. She let me in and asked the girls if any knew my sister. One of the girls said she did. I approached her and asked if she could tell my sister that I wanted to see her. The girl looked at me as if she knew that was not the real reason I was there. She smiled and agreed to tell my sister. She mentioned that I could do that myself at Town Hall.

I gathered up enough courage and blurted out that it was not fair that they got to live with their sisters, right next door to their brothers.

She stared at me intently for a while, then asked, "Do you know why we have to live here?"

I suspected it was because they were all the same color, but not sure. I stood there, not saying anything. She rolled up her sleeve and held out her arm. It was the same explanation given by the children playing outside Town Hall.

I reiterated, "I still do not believe it is fair you get to be with your sisters and brothers, just because your relatives are from Africa."

Their governess seemed to be laughing, although I believe she might have been crying. The girl stared at me for a while, then asked, "Can I give you a kiss?" I was about eight years old, had agreed with my friends we hated girls, and was getting a kiss from a girl — not good! However, I agreed she could if it was kept a secret.

A couple of years later, those in charge of the living arrangements must have heard our complaints. Ours was about preferential treatment. The Division 10 and 11 complaints were very different. Interesting enough, it was about the time when the Supreme Court decided there was no such thing as separate and equal. The Division 10 and 11 children were placed into the divisions with us other children. For all of us it was a fairness issue, though for different reasons.

PRIDE

Reasons children found themselves in the home were blind to all that made them different, save perhaps poverty. Exposure to the many diversities of other children allowed us to see differences just for what they were. Most carried this lesson with them for the rest of their lives. Children admitted to the home while toddlers were never exposed to many outside attitudes, such as bigotry. Some children admitted to the home at a later age carried such baggage. Subsequent exposure to the many diversities of the other children surely changed their attitudes.

One experience made me so proud of my siblings. During summer, those hearts too large sponsored a trip to a theme park down south. We stopped by a gas station to go to the bathroom. The owner said the white children could use the facility, but the black children, using a distasteful characterization, had to go out back. Without hesitation, we all went out back and pissed with our black brother. I still cry when I recall this memory.

13

The journal

Recollections of times and events long ago can be aided by something, someone, or a written record. I was never keen on remembering many of my home experiences, especially the bad ones. It was left to some written records to trigger recalls of these.

During a homecoming, we were notified that the south side boys' divisions would be torn down to save money on maintenance costs. These divisions were no longer needed due to declining enrollment. Before tearing them down, items left over from those divisions were placed in Division 14 for sale. Many years had been spent in those divisions. I went to see if there were some keepsakes. Most of the popular items had been taken. I noticed a box in the closet of the governess's room. It appeared to have been untouched. The box had several bundles of papers, each neatly bound with very colorful ribbons. The way they were bundled indicated they were very special to someone. Upon examining these papers, it became obvious they were daily records of the happenings in Division 14, including the time when I lived in that division. Reading those records was like watching reruns of TV shows; only now they were of my life. Both precious and unpleasant memories were recalled because of those records. I guess both the pleasant and unpleasant are part of us. Each need to be recalled for us to know what the whole of us once was, and what made us what we are today. I will narrate about those which dealt only with me and can be accurately recalled.

BAGGAGE

Children coming to the home at a very young age carried little baggage. Those joining at later ages carried much more. Some had baggage that no child should have to carry. This baggage influenced their behaviors. Some exhibited extreme behaviors. The children themselves inadvertently helped in hiding these behaviors from the oversight of the governesses. They adhered to that rule of rules. The children never told, never! A society cannot endure without establishing the means to control those who exhibit extreme behaviors. The children themselves created the most effective means to control their bad-acting siblings. The children threatened them with punishment children fear the most: isolation. Those who attempted their extreme agendas quickly found themselves alone among so many.

HANDLING BULLIES 101

That which has pervaded our society since the beginning of time was the most common extreme behavior. There were several strategies in dealing with bullies. As mentors, the older boys taught us what they believed was the best strategy. We were taught to hit back, get up when knocked down, then hit back harder. The objective was to inflict enough damage that bullies would think twice the next time. Unfortunately, a price had to be paid, and it was not pleasant spending the next few days with your entire body hurting. Other strategies were developed.

HANDLING BULLIES 201

For us unsuccessful with the lesson taught by our mentors, the most popular strategy I called "Avoid the Bullies." At the expense of insulting the reader, the objective was simply to avoid the bullies. This strategy was most effective right before meals. One half hour before meals, the governesses left their divisions to go eat. The children were left alone; bullies were alone with those they preyed upon. We who practiced the "Avoid the Bullies" strategy simply left the division immediately after waking up. We hid until the governesses came back. We were required to complete our chores during this time. As they were not, punishment was awaiting when we returned from hiding. Fortunately, the punishment was always demerits. It was better to be poor than suffer the pain from those bullies.

HANDLING BULLIES, CUSTOMIZED

A strategy for handling bullies was tailor made for me. An open field may be fun for playing. It does not offer any cover when a predator is around. This was especially true for us not blessed with quick of feet. If sufficient attention was not given to the surroundings, the preyed frequently found themselves in proximity of predators. One of my mentors gave me a strategy customized for us not quick of feet. He taught me to run just slow enough to let the bully get right behind me, which of course was no problem. I then quickly dropped to the ground. That wonderful property of momentum caused many a bully to tumble over my heap; often injuring themselves. I became so good at this that older boys would bet others they could catch me, but not actually catch me, if you know what I mean.

HANDLING BULLIES 301

The most advanced strategy was reserved for those exhibiting the most extreme bullying. They earned the attention of older children, especially when their brothers were the victims. These Guardian Angels made it known in no uncertain terms that extreme agendas would not be tolerated. One of the records in Division 14 attested to such an occurrence. It mentioned that one of the tougher children was beaten, possibly from an encounter with an older boy. I believe this unfolded right before my eyes. While leaving Division 14 to implement the "Avoid the Bullies" strategy, I came upon a Guardian Angel pinning a bully against the division wall. Using that which the bully practiced on us, he taught this bully a very painful lesson. His recommendation to the bully was to change his ways or get more of the same. The threat of receiving that which he sought to deal out was a very effective change mechanism. This bully not only changed his ways, he started teaching others how to defend themselves against bullies. After leaving the home, he was successful as a hero charged with defending our country. Perhaps Guardian Angels beget Guardian Angels.

HANDLING BULLIES, THE LAST RESORT

While working at the home, I and one fondly referred to as the enforcer became good friends. He indicated there was an item the home had in storage that he believed was mine, and one that he knew was mine. We went to an upstairs room in the administration building. The room was full of an astonishing collection of items.

Most were items that the parents had sent their siblings but had been stored because the children were not allowed to possess them. I saw more BB guns than could be counted, many from that immortal no youngster of today could possibly know, Red Ryder. There were also too many play guns to count; also from immortals many youngsters would not recognize. We children had played with similar guns. I asked the enforcer why they had kept those from the children. It was explained that they were kept from the children only if they were too realistic.

Other items were those the home no longer used. One section was full of old military uniforms and flags. Another section had huge pictures of the presidents that once hung on the classroom walls of Morton Memorial High School. There were many, many old pictures donated by individuals and organizations. There were signed pictures of movie stars, some signed baseballs, and I believe one signed football. Most noticeable were reels of film, movies taken by home staff of the events in the home. There were simply too many items to inventory in this story.

The enforcer retrieved a box with the initials "RC", along with a short message: "Did you lose something?" The box contained a knife. He explained that it had been taken from me while in Division 14. When he tried to return it upon graduation, I tossed it away. The governess retrieved it, and they kept it in storage. I told him the story behind that knife.

Many boys had knives, for very innocent purposes. One purpose not so innocent was to warn bullies to leave you alone. A friend advised me to get this equalizer. I followed his advice. I was a very good boy for a long time, getting no demerits. With the money saved, a knife was purchased at the 5 and 10 in a nearby town. Once bullies knew of this equalizer, they left me alone. However, one bully broke that unwritten rule. He told the governess about the knife. The knife was quickly confiscated. After losing the knife, this bully cornered me. I put my hand in my pocket as if I still had the knife. I warned the bully I would use it if I had to. Surprisingly, this bully smiled, gave me a look of approval, and left me alone. When I graduated from the home, my governess gave me a small box containing this knife, with the initials RC and the message "Did you lose something?" I thought it was too little, too late. I threw it away. Apparently, the governess retrieved it.

A Red Ryder BB gun was the item that the enforcer was unsure about. It was in an unopened box with an attached card which read, "For Ralph, Love Mom and Dad."

The enforcer told me I could not have it unless I could verify that it was mine. I told him I would ask my parents about it. On hindsight, I know of no other child that shared my first name. At the end of summer, I visited Mom and Dad before returning to college. I asked if they had sent me a Red Ryder BB gun. They indicated that they had, but the home told them children were not allowed to have them. They were told that the BB gun would be saved and given to me upon leaving.

WHERE DID THEY GO?

Many, many years later, I asked the enforcer about the BB gun. The enforcer took me to this same room where I had initially seen the BB gun. The room was nearly empty. He asked if I remembered when that room had been full of the children's items. I could see some tears in his eyes.

He told me many of those items just disappeared. I think about this BB gun every time I see that popular story about Christmas.

NEVER FORGET

By the time I entered the ninth grade, most of the extreme children had either changed their ways, or had left the home. I realized that some of my siblings, those that experienced the wrath of bullies, had outgrown their tormentors. It was no surprise those former bullies now sought their friendship. Well, at least they were not enemies. I never grew at all since junior high. Subsequently, I gained little to no respect from the bullies. I would like to blame the devil for what happened next. However; I may have to do time where he lives. I certainly do not want to piss him off. He would be proud of me though. Revenge was on my mind.

As an extremely small school, it was important for most of the high school boys to participate in football, just to have enough for a team. Thankfully, using that term loosely, this included some of the current and former bullies. Perhaps they wanted to play because that sport involved hitting others. One of my friends had shared my experiences with bullies when we were younger. He grew large enough, and mean enough, that he followed that philosophy of Jesus; somewhat altered. He did onto them what they had done upon him. I believe that he recognized my stature had not changed since junior high. I had no chance of doing what he could. During a football practice, he took me aside. He explained how I could gain some respect. I interpreted that as revenge. Several practice drills involved serious contact. Most of the players went half speed to avoid getting hurt. Not gifted with speed, but possessing considerable coordination, I singled out my former bullies, and delivered some hurt. Though painful to myself also, the satisfaction of revenge far outweighed any pain. Sorry! After a few weeks of practice, the coach took me aside and told me some of the children complained that I was too rough during practice. He reminded me it was only a game. Well, that was his opinion. I stopped however. After all, we needed them for the team. One good outcome was that I had very few problems with bullies after I started participating in sports.

BEING A BULLY

The enforcer and I not only were good friends. We attended college together, both taking courses for a master's degree. While we were eating at the student center, he recalled an incident when I attempted bullying. He let me know that the home staff had a very good laugh about that. I told him I had learned a valuable lesson from that experience.

Knowing bullies and being abused by them seems to have the effect of creating bullies. I chose a larger boy on which to practice this distasteful practice. This boy had shown no hint of hitting back, and everyone hated him. We both worked in the kitchen. I ordered him to retrieve some potatoes, a chore I disliked. When he refused. I slapped him and threatened him with more of the same if he did not obey. I was a bully! Fortunately, as regards what lessons are well learned; or unfortunately, as regards how lessons are well learned; this kid took exception. He reared back and brought one from about the third row, a phrase learned from one of my siblings who became a very good boxer. I remember lying on the ground, with he who I attempted to bully standing over me. I asked what happened. In his painful simplicity, he explained that I hit him and he hit me back. My jaw still hurts! That was the extent of my bullying. I went back to being the bullied. That was much healthier. I hated this boy for a while, but I should have thanked him. He and my guardian angel must have had a good laugh. The home staff did.

14

Summer Camp

Summer camp was the favorite escape from life in the home. The camp was far from the home, surrounded by woods and a farming community. A small river made its way around two sides of the camp. The river's flood plain occupied the other two sides. Needless to say, we kept a close watch on the river and its flood plain when it downpoured. Three army-style barracks were used to house about twelve children each. Married couples served as camp counsellors, sharing a small cabin adjacent to the barracks. Back doors of the barracks and cabin were adjacent to the river; most convenient for the campers, if you know what I mean. While children scattered to the four corners of the earth during camp, healthy appetites, good food and dedicated cooks ensured one hundred percent participation at meal times.

A cherished bell signaled the children to be at the flag pole early in the morning. The bell can still can be seen at the camp. The day started with raising the flag, and repeating the pledge in record time, in anticipation of the one activity no one missed. After chores were done, it was every man for himself, a favorite phrase used by our loveable band director when we played the breakout string in one of those Sousa marches. Except for the planned, evening activities, we succumbed to the call of the wild. Nighttime was sleeping time for the counsellors. It was otherwise for the children. They found fishing spots, built a bonfire, and roasted hot dogs stolen from the kitchen. The cooks made sure there were plenty of those hot dogs to be had. We knew they knew, and they knew we knew, but it was sort of exciting to think we were getting away with something. The camp offered far more freedom than what the home allowed, becoming a special place for many.

Swimming, wading the river to catch turtles, frogs, snakes, and crawdads were common activities. Crawdad tails were removed, covered with mud, and tossed into a bonfire. Very tasty! Attempts to prepare fish resulted in a charcoal, burnt fish banquet. When not cooked on site, the cooks prepared any fish and frog legs. Once we caught a large groundhog. The cooks refused to cook it. We tried to cook it on a bonfire. That taught us why we relied on cooks. I hope the critters in those woods liked charcoaled groundhog. Everyone participated in planned activities in the evening. One evening was reserved for banana splits, and of course one for roasting hot dogs and marshmallows on a large bon fire. I made it known to the home staff that I would rather stay at the home in the summer and attend camp than go on vacation with volunteer families. There are too many stories about the camp to fit into this story. I will recall the most memorable.

RISK TAKERS

Risk takers were not rare at the home. The camp provided plenty of opportunities for them to push the envelope. I was not one, and I was certain a close friend shared that attribute. Was I wrong!

Two other creeks emptied into the small river running thru the camp, adding to the flow when the rains came. The winter thaw and the spring rains added to this flow. This seemingly innocent river turned into an extremely dangerous torrent. With all the obstacles in the river, even the most rugged of whitewater rafters would not dare challenge it. During one of these torrents, I was running along the cliff overlooking the river. I noticed a child being swept down the rapids. I grabbed a long stick and made my way down the sandy cliff to help. It was Harden, a good friend. Harden was one I never expected to take risks. He surely had fallen into the river. I made my way down next to the river, through a flooded area, right next to the torrent. I held out the stick and yelled for him to grab it. He ignored me! He was swept into a bend in the river where the torrent of water smashed into a very large tree. It was right next to the river. When it flooded, it was right in the path of the rapids. The water hit the tree, shot straight up high into the air, taking with it anything and anyone who happened to be in those rapids. Over the years, the river had washed the soil from under that tree, exposing a web of roots. These would act like iron bars of a jail, preventing escape by anyone or anything swept under those roots. It would be curtains.

Harden and the water hit that tree, both shooting high into the air. The water fell back in the rapids, making a splashing sound. Harden fell back in, yelling something unintelligible. He was immediately swept under the roots of that tree. Horrified, I made my way down into the river on the outside of those roots. I stuck the stick as far into the water under those roots as I could, hoping Harden would grab it. Realizing he did not, I let myself down further into the water, holding on to the roots. I chickened out on going under the water beneath those roots; something I regret to this day. Just as I thought all was lost, Harden's hands were seen on those roots, pulling himself from that watery grave. I helped him out, and we sat by the river, relieved he was okay.

After resting, Harden stood up. To my astonishment, he appeared like he was about to jump back into the river!

He looked at me and said, "Come on, it's fun."

I realized that he was in the river by design, not by accident.

Not being a risk taker, I nodded in the way that meant, "No way!"

Harden grabbed my hand, and into the rapids he and I went. Initially, I was mad about being forced into that murky water. That emotion was quickly replaced by the urgency to stay alive. Harden taught me how to body surf in those rapids, and most thankfully, how to stay alive. Unbeknownst to me, Harden liked to face that charging rhino.

I believe he became a protector after leaving the home, appropriately so. Although there were plenty of opportunities, I never body surfed down that river again. Some things should be done only once during a lifetime.

FLOODS AND BANANA SPLITS

The most memorable event at the camp was one that turned every child's fantasy into reality. The river had the nasty habit of rising very quickly when it rained. When it poured, it did not take much time for the river to make its way to the back door of our bunks. During one of these downpours, Bob got up to take a piss behind the bunk. As he stepped out the back door, we heard a splash followed by a scream. We ran to the door. Bob was holding onto a tree for dear life, preventing himself from being swept down the river. The water had risen right up to the back door of the bunk in a very short time! It continued to pour, and eventually the only dry spot was on top of the dining room tables. The camp counsellors called for a bus to evacuate us. The bus sent to evacuate us could not reach the camp grounds as the road into the camp was also flooded. The only way out was to wade down that flooded road, now waist deep with water.

It was a day planned for banana splits. One very thoughtful child instantly became extremely popular. He reminded the counsellors that the ice cream, bananas, and syrup would spoil, as there was no power. Those wonderful counsellors earned the admiration of all children on Earth. They told us to eat the ice cream and bananas! They never mentioned the syrup, but we improvised. The scene was about thirty-six children stuffing themselves with ice cream and syrup, peeling bananas and eating them. This done while wading down the road out of the camp. It was a very weird evacuation. The banana peels were recycled, food for the critters. For years, we found those ice cream containers along the river bank.

SOME JUST DO

As we neared the bus, we encountered some very fast rapids across the road. A flooded area was emptying itself through the woods, across the road, and into the river. It was too fast and too deep for the smaller children to attempt a crossing. The counsellors had a great idea. We obtained a large rope. Sections of the rope were wrapped around the waists of the larger children. The smaller children then held on to the rope as we crossed those rapids. It was an event that would reveal the difference between those that think about acting, and those that just do.

As we were crossing, one of the smaller children could not hold on. Down the rapids he went. He screamed, as did many of us. Most of us wanted to help, but the expectation of death prevented that. One of the two no-nonsense kids reacted quickly. Without thinking about the danger, he went down the rapids, grabbed the child, and brought him back to the rope. I was astonished at what he had done. At the same time, I was ashamed that I had not reacted like that. Those feelings did not distract from my sense for survival however. I stayed very close to this doer while we traversed those rapids.

15

The Woods Game

Just as the woods at the camp was a wonderful playground, so were the woods surrounding the home. A permit and buddy system was used to allow children to visit the woods. That was the ivory tower rule. The practical rule was children could go to the woods if they were not caught sneaking to and from. The staff knew the temptation was too great. Most ignored us breaking that rule. At most, punishment was usually very unkind words. Going to the woods was the perfect escape from the regimental existence at the home. In our birthday suits we swung from a rope into a small swimming hole. The girls went there to participate in the same activities as the boys. One of my girl homies confessed to me that they spied on the boys as they swam. Unbelievable!

Most what I created at the home lacked normality. One game I created bordered on insanity. The game was to run as fast as possible through the woods, as if it were a matter of life or death. Any obstacles encountered were dealt with quickly. Many of these obstacles objected to being interrupted and dealt out punishment. Despite this punishment, I continued to run. The beaten path was avoided. It offered no challenges. When there was a choice between a safe path and one with unknown consequences, the latter was always chosen. When encountering a hill, I continued down or up as fast as I could. I often fell, injuring myself. When encountering bushes with thorns, I attempted to run straight through. Well, I did the first time. Extremely dangerous excursions, such a cliff, were avoided. I was insane, not stupid. Crossing a river was no challenge, except when it flooded. This small river turned into very dangerous white-water. Attempts to cross this confirmed the insanity of this game. The body surfing lessons learned from Harden proved invaluable and saved me from some unsatisfactory fates. My closest brush with death happened when I encountered some branches that had fallen into the river. For any that may be reading this, never underestimate the force of flowing water. That force swept me under those branches. I was pinned against the branches and the bottom of the river. I quickly learned that the river was not that deep. Bracing myself against the bottom and those branches, a hard push found my head above water. I made a very bad mistake in believing I could do this any time. I was wrong! I managed to be swept under some branches in a deep part of the river. Pushing up did not find my head above water. I panicked, and attempted to climb on top of those branches. As only luck could guarantee, I managed to get one leg over a large branch, allowing me to escape from the grave. I avoided these obstacles in the future. As mentioned before, I was insane, not stupid.

There were many sprained ankles, thorns in just about every part of my body, scratches, bruises; you get the picture. On more than one occasion, it took a long time to recuperate. One experience was a stark reminder of how I could end up participating in this insanity. I was running thru an old graveyard adjacent to the home. It had very tall, beautiful monuments, many that had fallen. As weird as it may seem, I managed to run into an open grave. It was well hidden with branches and leaves, just waiting for someone with my insanity. Why there was an open grave, I have no idea. I could hardly move from that sudden stop on the bottom of that grave. I laid there for the better part of the evening. My sides hurt so much I could not stand up. I became nauseated. After the pain lessened, I realized how ridiculous my predicament was. It made me laugh, adding to the pain. I had ended up exactly where one would when the envelope is pushed too far. All my siblings had to do was to shovel in the dirt, and place one of those fallen monuments on it, with the words, "He was insane - not stupid"! After some time, I noticed that there was a tunnel on one side of the grave. It was as if the occupant of that open grave had tunneled out. Very strange! I managed to crawl through the tunnel. It led to another empty grave! Fortunately, this grave was dug out so much it was easy to crawl out. Later I found out some of my homies were using those opened graves as their home away from home. They dug out tunnels from one open grave to another. How weird is that! I continued to crawl thru the graveyard, trying to get near the highway to flag down a car. Crawling gave a view of the surroundings much like a dog would see. It was *wood dark*, causing a rude introduction to many of the monuments. Several were statues of angels, causing me to wonder why my guardian angel was avoiding my situation. I made it to the highway and waited for a car. One never came. The hospital was not far and I crawled there. This extremely old nurse came out and helped me inside. She checked me out and said it appeared I had just cracked some ribs. She called a doctor who confirmed the cracked ribs. I spent the night there and went back to the division the next morning. The governess told me they initially thought I had run away when I did not show up for supper. When I told her the truth about what happened, she had that all too familiar look of disbelief. Understandably! There surely are not many experiences out there that describe a night in a grave.

If anyone wants to try the woods game, don't. Especially where there are bulls. The punishment was many times extremely harsh, sometimes with injuries that took weeks to heal. In hindsight, I was extremely lucky to escape serious injuries, or even worse. There seemed to be an intoxicating excitement about meeting the challenges of these obstacles and surviving. Perhaps I had learned that lesson as a risk-taker from Harden.

DANCING WITH BULLS

I mentioned not to go where there are bulls. During this strange game, I found myself running thru a meadow. I stepped in several of those little surprises, evidence that the area belonged to those responsible for the wonderful dairy products. While messy, those encounters weren't as pressing as the concern about the guardian of that meadow. The farmer had provided a bull for the ladies, one that saw fit to enforce a no trespassing policy. It was a small bull. Thankfully, the farmer had had its horns stubbed, possibly out of consideration for us children.

A sense of urgency came over me when I felt the breath of this bull near my butt. I realized the penalty for entering his domain was surely the same seen in old movies of bull fights. You know, the ones where matadors are the unfortunate losers. Running, dodging, and praying kept this adversary at bay. It soon became evident that praying would soon be my only recourse. A meadow offers no place to hide. Lacking quick of feet ensured the bull would soon enforce its policy. Acting more from instinct, I stopped, turned around and faced my adversary. The bull seemed more surprised by this than I. He also stopped. As we faced each other, he gave me that look most puppies give you when you do something stupid. The bull started swinging its head. I thought this was funny as its horns were not hitting anything. It ceased to be funny when the bull charged, catching me in the behind and sending me through the air in what only can be described as some strange aerial acrobatics. I would now like to express sincere appreciation to the farmer for getting a small bull, and most certainly for stubbing its horns. The back of that bull broke my fall. I fell off, right on my butt. Who says a big and soft butt is not desirable.

Fright and confusion seem to be good companions. The former told me to run. The latter told me to run right towards the bull. I grabbed the tail of this guardian of the meadow. The bull turned around and around. I followed, holding onto its tail. I quickly surmised it would be much healthier to face the ass of the bull than its horns. At times, I could not hold on, but the bull was turning so quickly that it overran me. I waited until its behind came back around, grabbed its tail, and around and around we went. After some time performing this strange waltz, the bull stopped. I could hear very loud breathing, both mine and the bull's. I thought the bull was giving up! I released its tail and started to run. My favorite friend, curiosity, forced me to stop and glance at the bull. We both stood there staring at each other, both panting hard. I had this strange sensation of wanting to do what nowadays is referred to as a high five. I made an alternate, much wiser choice. I turned around and continued to run through the woods. I never went into that meadow again. Some things in life you should do only once.

A BLOODY MESS

The wounds I received from one of the tumbles in those woods resulted in one of my best pranks, although its outcome was unexpected. I encountered a steep hill. As always, I ran down at full speed. I fell, experiencing a hurt long remembered. The farmer had cut down a barbed wire fence and left it lying on the hill. Don't they know about us woods runners! The human flesh is not designed to endure those barbs. The entire front of my chest was bloody from sliding along that barbed wire. They were not life-threatening cuts, but many, many of them. I returned to the home with this bloody chest. I passed by Town Hall where the girls were dancing. It was one of those rare instances when a prank simply presents itself and the temptation is too great. I hid behind a bush near a window where the girls were dancing. I peeked out and threw some stones to get the attention of one of the girls standing by the window. I told her to get some other girls, as I had something to show them. Her look and reply confirmed what I and certainly others always suspected about myself, which I took no exception. However, her curiosity got the better of her and several others. In hindsight, they probably were expecting something very different than what I planned. I stepped out from behind the bush and showed my bloody chest. The girls simply said the blood was ketchup and ignored me. Rats!

16

Unmemorable Memories

SEXUAL PREDATORS

We would like to forget some memories. However, all make up our total being. We must deal with both. While good memories are readily recalled, it takes something or someone to unveil the bad memories. Such was the case while reading the papers neatly bundled in Division 14, daily records of the happenings there. One referred to an encounter between two children, one very innocent, and the other not so innocent. The record stated a child had injured another who tried to take a shower with him. It was an obvious reference to an experience of a friend. We will call him Ninja One.

Showers and baths were optional, at least until we did not pass the smell test. While Ninja One was taking a shower, a much larger boy entered and grabbed him from behind. He had one arm around Ninja One's waist and the other over his mouth. Ninja One was about to experience something no young child should. Fortunately, one of our own was a student of the art of defense. He was more than eager to share his expertise. One defensive maneuver he taught was idea for Ninja One's predicament. Ninja One lifted his legs and placed both feet behind each of the predator's ankles. With a quick sweep of his feet, and a wet shower floor to assist, the larger boy ended up on the shower floor and Ninja One on top of him. The larger boy could have been ruined for life. We could only hope. While Ninja One adhered to that rule of rules, I did not. Attempting to hide my handwriting, I left a note for the governess.

INSENSITIVITY

It is seldom that we get the chance to encounter those who have treated us badly in an earlier life. We seem to avoid each other. Such an encounter happened. At a homecoming about thirty years after graduating, I encountered a person about my age. Age disguises who we once were. It also serves as a good indicator we may have met long ago. We introduced ourselves. He asked if I remembered him. I told him I remembered him. I also told him of the experience Ninja One had related to me. I saw his eyes watering. He turned around and walked away. My disgust of him changed to disgust of myself. I had reminded him of something that happened when he had been a troubled child. The home had few, if any, programs to counsel children like him. It was possible he had changed, only to be reminded by one so insensitive. We all lived in a glass house, and I had cast stones at his. I never again approached any of my siblings in a similar manner.

Ninja One's experience certainly was terrifying to him. It was also terrifying to me. I overreacted. I never again took showers or baths in the divisions when there were other children around. Other children and home staff complained that I was always smelly. I did shower at school after gym, but only after the other children were done. Even in the later years when I played sports, I avoided taking showers until the other children were done. This was completely unnecessary; however, the expectation that history will repeat itself dooms us to behavior we otherwise would not exhibit.

17

A Very Good Vacation

One of the descriptions of daily events in Division 14 mentioned that a priest had volunteered to take five of us on vacation. It was easy to recall this memory as this vacation was perfect. Children were chosen for vacations in the summer. Five of us were the unchosen ones. I had always refused to go on vacations alone because of a previous experience. This vacation would be different, as some of my siblings would be with me. The vacation was a dream come true for children our age. Aside from a requirement to sing during the church services, the couple left us completely alone, with a capital C and A.

Not of angelic character, we and the town constable quickly became friends. One of those with us had brought to the home considerable expertise in stealing. He offered to share it. We refused to involve ourselves in that, especially since we were surely on the constable's list. However, our expert thief explained we would just pretend to steal. Well, it was something to do. Off to the five and ten cents store we went to practice. We were taught how to pick something up, palm it, and pretend to put it back in its bin.

After this pretense to steal, we went back to the house, sharing stories of what we could have taken. In the driveway was the now familiar sheriff's car! With a lot of trepidation, we entered the house. The priest, his wife, store owner, and the sheriff were not smiling. The sheriff lined us up and explained that the owner of the store had seen us stealing. We tried to explain that we were just playing around and did not actually take something. That fell on deaf ears. The sheriff informed us that if we just admitted to the theft, we would not go to jail. He then started with the first in line, took him aside, and asked if he had stolen something. The threat of jail certainly influenced the answers.

I was the last in line. This gave me and my guardian angel time to contemplate what could be said in our defense. What transpired was certainly the fault of my guardian angel. I could never have thought of this. My question, oops, I mean the guardian angel's question, was obvious. Why would the sheriff be asking us to admit to stealing if he knew the answer? Aha, my conclusion, oops, I mean the guardian angel's conclusion, was that he was lying. The store owner never actually saw us take anything. It was my turn in line. The sheriff asked me if I had stolen something. To the astonishment of him, the priest and his wife; I answered "No!" Their jaws simultaneously hit the ground. Some of my siblings had the same reaction.

Now, sheriffs have probably gone through this scenario thousands of times, so they can recognize when children tell non-truths. The sheriff stared intently at me eye to eye. I was confident in the truthfulness of my response and stared right back. The sheriff grinned ever so slightly, turned around, and told the store owner, priest, and his wife that they needed to talk. Later, the priest came in and said God would be the judge of those who had sinned and would deal out appropriate punishment. That was certainly okay with us. We spent the rest of the vacation keeping out of trouble. It was too close a call.

18

My Siblings

ecause I lived with my siblings for so long, I had a good idea of what they were about. Many had qualities I wished to possess. To be like them, I took notice of what they did. After many years of this, it appears that parts of me became the same of those siblings. Most that I have become, I owe to these siblings. Of course, some had interesting qualities that did not become a part of me; and I am sticking with that story.

OUR SECRET AGENT

One interesting sibling was the same who had taught us to steal without stealing. We will give him one of those interesting names, Agent One. The track coach for Morton Memorial worked with me at the paint shop during the summer. We became good friends and shared stories of the times at the home. After telling him the story about stealing without stealing, the conversation migrated to Agent One. The track coach related that after Agent One left the home, some men came to discuss him. They were considering hiring him because of his special talents, and a lifestyle that the rest of their men could not duplicate without being made as agents. I told coach about one of his many talents.

Upon living with each other for many years, there were no secrets who the usual suspects were when our stuff became missing. Recovering our stuff was extremely simple, at least if Agent One was your friend. The process was simply to have Agent One pick the lock on the lockers of these usual suspects. I had stuff stolen, but very few not recovered.

The extent of Agent One's talent was obvious when he accompanied our basketball team to a newly constructed school. The school was so new that keys to the dressing rooms had not been distributed. We and the opposite team found ourselves sitting in the gym, waiting for someone to unlock the locker room doors. Some of us jokingly said we should pick the locks. The coach from the opposite team told us to forget about picking them. They were state of the art. Now that challenge could not be ignored by you know who. Agent One asked us to keep our coach busy and commenced to pick those state-of-the-art locks. Our coach appeared not to be surprised at this. He asked Agent One to help the other team, which he did. They could at least have said thanks. I believe they may have changed their locks immediately after the game. I know for a fact they never scheduled us again.

OUR BRAVE ONE

Another sibling had a quality that is admired by all. It was one of those qualities that I unsuccessfully tried to duplicate. Perhaps it is one that either you do or do not have. We will call him John. He was the same child who had rescued another from being swept down the rapids while walking out of the flooded camp. He exhibited another example of bravery, told to me by some children who had witnessed it. The river in the woods next to the home had turned into raging rapids. When these rapids approached branches over the river, they simply made a small opening through the branches. Water shot out of that opening, high into the air. Anything in the river would share that fate, including children. The game was to dive into the river, into the branches, then enjoy being shot up into the air.

Only the bravest did this, or as far as we cowards were concerned, the stupidest. If one were trapped under those branches with that raging water, it would be certain death. Such did happen. As everyone stood around wondering what to do, John quickly dove in and rescued the trapped child. What was interesting about this was John and this other child were not friends. John had an attribute all of us wished we had. It was a good example of how each child is unique and each has attributes that others do not. I had learned this a long time before this act of bravery.

19

The Best Lesson

The best lesson is without a doubt one that is realized thru experience. While going thru those bundled papers of the daily happenings in Division 14, I came upon one that read "One boy was punished for destroying a book titled *Little Black Sambo*" The memory of this I knew ever so well.

We all had nicknames. Some we did not like. Divisions 18 and 19 were not used to house children because of declining enrollment. They were used for overnight stays of the alumni during homecoming. During one homecoming, I went over to Division 18 to search for a sister who had graduated the previous year. I never found her. I did find a very pretty garment. It was purple, red and blue, with white fluffy trim and a very wide belt. I put it on and proudly wore this newly found gem to school. Everyone was laughing! One of the older girls took me aside and told me it was a girl's thing and most certainly not for boys. I took it off. My so-called buddies did not let me forget this embarrassment. They created several nicknames that I hated.

I believe my siblings felt sorry for me, as those nicknames disappeared, much to my liking. Unfortunately, events unfurled that would revisit one of those nicknames. Daniel and I were reading the story *Little Black Sambo*. Daniel had dark skin, which I mention only because it is related to this story. After reading the story, I told Daniel I would nickname him *Little Black Sambo*. Daniel looked at me in a way that made me believe one of my insensitivities had encountered one of his sensitivities. Daniel objected, telling me it was wrong to nickname someone based on their color. Ignorant as I was, I saw nothing wrong with that. Daniel challenged me. He agreed that I could call him *Little Black Sambo* if I allowed everyone to call me by a nickname he created. I accepted the challenge. Daniel chose the name *Girtie*, most certainly from that moment in my life when I had worn the pretty garment to school. I objected to *Girtie*. Daniel reminded me of our agreement. We told everyone our nicknames. After about three days of everyone laughing at me, I begged Daniel to call off the challenge. I admitted that he had won. Daniel refused until I bribed him with a sweater of mine that he liked. The children stopped calling Daniel *Little Black Sambo*. They continued to call me *Girtie* for years to come. From that time on, I was very careful about referring to children based on their characteristics.

20

Girls

THE CONUNDRUM

Morton Memorial was enjoying an era when their sports programs were tremendous. The team's successes motivated us younger ones to practice. Every other night, from about six to eight in the evening, everyone of junior and high school age could go to this wonderful, cherished activity center: Town Hall. Town Hall had an old gym where we boys practiced, to attain that Hoosier dream. Town Hall also had rooms adjacent to the gym where the boys and girls could get together. Hence the obvious conundrum. While at that age we were supposed to ignore girls, there was a waiting list to play in the game of basketball. Later, when the boy's hormones hit turbo, it became difficult to get enough boys to make up basketball teams. Eventually three on three games became popular. To the rescue came a group dedicated to saving the game, The Bachelor's Club.

I was voted president, the only time I was ever president of anything, or even voted for anything. It made me very proud. I took great pride in the club's mission, which was to save our Hoosier dream; i.e. to focus on basketball and not the girls. Somehow, Becky and I became best friends. I suppose that would make here my first girlfriend. I was walking out of our class together, my arm around her shoulder! When we got to the hallway, the remnants of the basketball team, oops, I mean the bachelor club, were staring at us.

One appropriately said, "He likes girls!"

I was voted out of the bachelor's club but allowed to remain on the basketball team, probably because I was the only one who could navigate thru the bulges on the Town Hall gym floor while dribbling.

LOVE REVEALS ITSELF

One very pretty girl in the fifth grade sent obvious signals that she liked me. We will refer to her as Sister. Let us recapitulate. Within two years, one girlfriend got me expelled from the bachelor's club, and Sister liked me. Not bad, two girl friends in one year! That she liked me was revealed from a game we played at recess. At that age, she was hands down the fastest runner of both the girls and boys. Likewise, I was absolutely the slowest; sad enough, of both boys and girls. We played this game in which one child was designated as the It. The It had to tag others. Each one tagged joined the It in tagging the others. The game ended when everyone had been tagged. It was advantageous to choose the slowest runner as the first It, which is when I come into the picture. I seldom participated. It was not fun spending recess chasing the others. Sister was never chosen as the It as she would quickly catch the next fastest, making the game very short. Additionally, she reveled in making sure the first one caught would be a boy. Some of the boys were terrified of this. Being the compassionate ones we were, we would not let him forget he had been caught by a girl.

To avoid my usual boring recess, I decided to play. I was quickly designated as the It Miraculously, I easily caught Sister, and the game ended very quickly. This was repeated several times. Funny how love reveals itself! Without saying goodbye, she left the home. Rumors flew that her parents had given her the choice to remain at the home or join a convent to become a nun. She chose the convent. Let us recapitulate. She had the choice of staying at the home as my girlfriend or becoming a nun. She chose a nun. Hum!

SUE

My story would not be complete without discussing the love of my life. Most of the girls at the home were the love of my life, at least in my dreams. Sue was one I actually had a shot at. I will relate one very fond memory of this angel.

Sue was alluring, extremely intelligent, and had those attributes boys of our age considered admirable. She could discuss just about anything, although that was not important. All girls learn at an early age how to convey messages to get the attention of the boys. Thank God for that. We boys had no clue. A smile, a look, a simple "hi", was interpreted like, "She likes me!", regardless of how they intended. Sue did not need makeup. That no-makeup look made her appear even more seductive. She laughed when she was supposed to, at least as far as we boys were concerned. She could look at you like you were the only person in the room, and made you believe that you were. With her big brown eyes, she melted all that looked at her. To many, she was the most tantalizing creature at the home. Sue reminded me of that chocolate bar I stole from my Mother's purse. I do not know any boy that could refuse a piece of that sweetness.

It was near summer when she directed her tentacles in my direction. At that age, I was usually, smelly, dirty, and lacked any resemblance of a conversationalist. Now that I think about it, I have not changed any. Oh well! Lacking all that girls probably thought important, I wondered why this angel was giving this dreg of the earth any attention at all. But with my hormones such as they were, her smile was all it took for me to ask her to "Go with me." That she agreed is to this day the most surprising moment of my life. That summer was one of bliss, at least to myself. We held hands, kissed when we could, held each other close enough to get a good feel, and had lots of fun. Town hall was the only place we could intermingle. It was the main activity center at the home. One activity was listening to the beginnings of rock and roll played on an old Wurlitzer juke box. Sue got me out on the dance floor. Quite a feat when one realizes I was without dance. However; I was not without coordination. I told her I was afraid I would make a fool of myself in front of my friends. She convinced me that most of my friends were on vacation for the summer, and they would not see us. I trusted Sue one hundred percent. So out on the dance floor I went. Sue punched J7 on the juke box. It was a song called At The Hop. Sue convinced me that this song had a specific dance associated with it. She wanted to teach me that dance. Like I said, I trusted Sue to a fault. I spent the next few days learning that dance. It was a lot of fun.

Deep within all of us is another us. I must say, for some it is not that deep. That other us has all the ingredients necessary to plan tricks on others, especially the unsuspecting. They are the ingredients of the recipe to be a good pranker, thanks Amos and Andy. Being a good pranker, it was very difficult for me to be the prankee, thanks again Amos and Andy. It would take the most cunning of prankers to pull off one on this expert pranker.

The summer was over. My friends had come back from their vacations. We were all in the dance room at Town Hall. Sue played that song we had enjoyed that summer. She told me this would be a good time to show everyone that dance. I was excited! When I tried to pull her out on the dance floor with me, she complained that her ankle was twisted. She begged me to do the dance anyway. She convinced me my friends would be impressed. Did I mention I trusted her one hundred ten percent. Out on the dance floor I went. I started doing the dance Sue and I had practiced. The room was very noisy when I started that dance. Everyone was telling others of their summer vacation experiences. After a couple of minutes making those dance moves, they began to take notice. The room got quieter, quieter and then silent. I realized my friends were being impressed with my coordination, and that dance move. I glanced at Sue. She gave me the thumbs up. I continued. The laughing started quietly at first, built up gradually, and eventually was full blast. I stopped and looked around at my friends. They were bending over laughing! At first I was disappointed they did not appreciate the dance. Then lightning struck! I glanced over at Sue. She was also laughing, at me I might add. I realized I had been pranked! I moved towards Sue to voice my displeasure. She headed for the girl's bathroom. I was so mad that I almost went in after her. I finally made a mad dash from Town Hall to my division.

I fumed for the better part of the night. Some of my so called friends complimented me on my dance moves. Their honesty in that was unmistakable. They could not help but laugh. As I was lying in bed that night, I contemplated what had taken place. Sue planned very carefully. She used her wiles to gain my trust. With that trust she convinced me to do that stupid dance. She thrust a dagger into my heart. To say I fell for it hook, line and sinker would not do that phrase justice. Being one to appreciate a good prank, I started laughing. I laughed so hard that I started tearing. One of my friends in the bed next to me thought I was crying. He tried to console me. He told me the dance was not all that bad. He then broke out laughing. That made me laugh even harder, and cry even more.

I take my hat off to my homies. They are amazing. Just as I salute Fred, that super frog, every homecoming; I also look towards the girls living quarters and give a salute to Sue. I loved her even more after that prank. I think we could have been lovers forever more at the home. But young girls are like the words to a song I remember every so well, Run Around Sue. And they should be. If she is reading this, I never stopped loving you.

MY LAST GIRLFRIEND

The relationship of my last girlfriend at the home turned out to be by far the most interesting, if you know what I mean. Before we get to her part in this story, there was an incident, years earlier, that puts an ironic twist to this story.

Two of my friends in the fifth grade hated each other. Their conversations quickly degraded into name calling. Their hand signals were definitely not hi or goodbye. I was very familiar with the intensity of their arguments. During math class, Natalie sat in front of me and Harland in back. This made me the equivalent of the pony express as these two expressed their feelings using that age-old process of passing notes during class. Getting those notes was like passing by an accident. I just had to look.

After a few weeks, it just got to be too much. I decided to play a joke on them. Harland gave me a note to pass to Natalie. It was his usual praise. I discarded that note and wrote another, attempting to duplicate his handwriting. It expressed how sorry he was about all those nasty things he had said, and that he would like to be friends. Natalie passed a note back, responding she would not fall for that trick, then made the usual suggestion on what he could do. I tried to duplicate her handwriting and passed a slightly altered note to Harland. This note passing increased, both in quantity and niceness; with a little help from a friend. After a while, there was no need to alter those notes at all. In fact, by the end of the class, their notes resembled what two lovers would express when getting together after an extended absence. I was somewhat concerned, as I believed they would disown me after they found out who was responsible for all that niceness. I kept a watch on them as they went out into the hall. They ended up walking down the hall, holding hands and laughing with each other. It seemed like they were deeply in love! I was in shock, asking myself, "What just happened?" I never told them what I did, at least when they were in the home. They remained friends for the rest of their time together at the home.

Years later, while a senior, a note appeared in the ink well on my desk. The desks were the old kind, with ink wells for of course, ink bottles. They were now ideal places to leave a note. The note was from a girl who previously never indicated an interest in me, nor I her. I cannot recall the exact words in the note. It indicated she was not going with anyone, and asked if I would like to go with her. For all you youngsters, "Go with you.", meant being girlfriend and boyfriend. Back in those days, it was acceptable for boys to ask the girls to go with them, never the opposite. Getting that note raised a red flag, although not very high. She was a fair maiden and my hormones were making all the decisions. I wrote a note back; expressing concern that we did not know each other very well. I asked two of my friends sitting between us to pass the note to her. I got a note back explaining that she had liked me for a long time but was afraid to ask me to be her boyfriend. We continued to write notes, having the other children in the class to pass them back and forth. Each time, her note was more intimate than the previous. It was one of the most exciting times in school, if you know what I mean.

I finally got a note asking if I would meet her at the hospital that evening right after supper. The quickness of that intimate invitation raised the *really* flag a lot higher. However, as I said before; my hormones were making all the decisions. After class, I met her at the water fountain. I asked when she wanted to meet at the hospital. She looked at me as if she had no idea what I was talking about, but she agreed to meet me. We then made plans to meet each other by the hospital after supper.

I was somewhat apprehensive that she seemed to be unaware of her invitation. I had this feeling that she and my friends were setting me up for a prank. However; as said before, my hormones were making all the decisions. The hospital was idea for dating. It was surrounded by thick bushes, and it had an ideal location. It was adjacent to the girl's divisions. Sneaking to the hospital was unnecessary because of a trick taught to me by, of all boys, Harland. One just had to make a cut on the arm, show some blood, and the governesses would immediately write out a permit to go to the hospital. Normally, the hospital would be avoided like the plague; however, location, location, location. I cut my arm, and the governess did exactly what she needed to do.

After receiving that awful mercurochrome treatment, I made my way around the side of the hospital. I did not expect to see this girl. I heard her call my name, and there she was, well hidden behind the bushes right next to the hospital. I went into the bushes, half expecting some of my friends to spring up, laughing that I had fallen for the prank. After realizing it was not a prank, I expressed some concern that other girls might see us. She told me that one of her friends was keeping watch for us. What happened next required little conversation and erased all doubt that it was a prank. It was by far the most revealing moment of my life, at least in the home. This happened with only about two weeks of my leaving the home, so we never had the chance to get together like before. Now I can explain the ironic part of this story.

Many years after graduating from the home, I contacted Harland. He liked those old country bars; the ones that you could toss shells from the nuts onto the sawdust on the floor. We listened to country music, drank, talked to the girls, and reminisced. After a few to many, I confessed to him about changing the notes with Natalie in the seventh grade. Harland laughed loudly, pounding the table. I was taken back at that extreme response. I told him it was not that funny. He shook his head and told me he was not laughing at that.

He asked if I remembered a girl who asked me to meet her at the hospital. I responded that I did. I asked how he knew that. He asked if I could recall who was passing the notes back and forth between us in class. I had that "Oh my God." feeling. We both laughed. Harland explained how he had made those notes. We had another drink.

Harland looked at me intently and asked, "Did you really believe this girl would agree to meet you?"

By that time, I was way past 'too many.' I told Harland that we indeed did meet. Harland's response was "Really?" followed with a look of doubt as to my truthfulness. We toasted our drinks. I then told Harland what happened during our meeting. Harland had a look that told me he was experiencing that same feeling I had when he and Natalie had walked down the hall holding hands. We both laughed and had another drink. I cannot remember the rest of the night, or the next day for that matter.

20

Mentors

Despite teacher's salaries being the lowest possible, Morton had some surprisingly very good teachers, a testimony that money itself cannot buy good teachers. Some were also very good mentors.

The strongest subject of our sixth-grade teacher was a history of hopefully the last world war. He was a veteran of that war, and one deeply involved in combat. If we sixth graders wanted a rest from the reading, writing, and arithmetic, one of us would mention the war. That was all it took for him to start off on a tangent with war stories. Children our age could never fully understand the horrors or the glory of that war. However, we were mesmerized by his recollections, and were at first were always quick to ask for more stories. It did not take long for us to recognize the pain he felt from that war. After a few horrific stories, he walked over to the windows. With his back towards us, he became silent as he gazed out over the school playground. Surely that playground was far different than what he visualized. It was an experience that he wanted, but could never, forget. His tears and the trembling in his voice told us of the pain that would not go away. We quit asking for those war stories. Another endearing aspect of this teacher was his ability to encourage children to participate in activities.

YOU DON'T KNOW UNTIL YOU TRY

Most of us boys played softball during recess. Those with no initiative never bothered to compete. Our sixth-grade teacher had a philosophy. You never know what you can or cannot do, until you try. He woke me from my recess nap to try softball. Well, my girlfriend had left for the monastery, and I had absolutely nothing to do. He started me out as catcher. The game seemed simple enough. One just had to catch the ball thrown by the pitcher, throw it back, and catch any balls fouled by the batter. I proceeded to toss the ball back to the pitcher so fast that he complained. I proceeded to catch all foul balls - I mean all of them, including some that were over the infield. Others complained that I caught too many, resulting in a very short time at bat. Over the next few weeks he had me play every position, except first base. They all were a piece of cake, so to speak. Finally, I was placed at shortstop, a position I excelled in for rest of my years at the home. Because of this teacher's ability to motivate, I found out that I could play baseball! After that, I started playing other sports, some which I excelled at during my stay at the home. What a wonderful teacher and mentor!

21

A Most Endearing Quality

One of the records describing the events in Division 14 alluded to a new child who had been punished for leaving the division and seeing his sisters. This referred to Billie, admitted to the home at about the age eleven. As with all children from loving parents, he held on to that hope of hopes for a long time. I believe that this hope was directly related to an endearing quality that most homies possess. One event illustrated this quality in a very strange way.

Billie and I graduated from the home in the same year. He showed up at my apartment about three years after graduating from the home. It was about three in the morning, and Billie showed signs of celebrating all night. After the usual "Hi, how are you"? and other rudimentary welcomes, he came directly to the point. He wanted to go out with a girl whom I had adored while at the home. He never mentioned her name. He wanted my permission! I adored about all the girls, so the exact identify of the one who he referred was not important. I just said it was OK. After he left, I thought about what had just happened. I realized that of all the things Billie valued, and for that matter many of my siblings, loyalty topped the list. I recalled an event that illustrated his outlook on loyalty.

About three years after Billie was admitted to the home, one of his parents came to visit. I just happened to be close by and saw Billie get out of a car. He was in tears. He ran towards our division while his parent yelled for him to come back. Later Billie revealed that this parent had remarried and bought a new car. Additionally, his spouse had on what appeared to be very expensive clothes. Billie had told his parent that if he/she could afford all of that, then he/she could afford to take him out of the home! From that point on, when his parent came to visit, Billie asked one of us to go with him to the woods. I am not sure Billie ever talked to that parent again.

22

The Worst of Times

The records in that bundle of papers in Division 14 related that a child had been punished for helping one of the older children bring in the cows for milking. It brought back a very painful memory.

I seemed to have been a loner. My siblings were willing to be friends. Though I shared that willingness, the how seemed to be lacking. It was one of those circular effects that spun out of control. I wanted to make friends but could not. Because I could not, I never had friends. Consequently, I wanted even more to have friends. This made me vulnerable to a much older boy, one who knew all too well how to recognize desperate children, and take advantage of their desperations. He was a true predator. He gave me candy and pop, engaged in complimentary conversations, and promised to protect me against bullies. I became very fond of him.

One of his chores was to bring in cows for milking. He told me I could go with him. This was very exciting. When it was time to get the cows, we went to a pasture behind the older boys' divisions. I ran around herding the cows, believing they were following my instructions. They gave me a quick glance, and continued grazing. He convinced me to take a rest, and we went to a small secluded area well out of sight from the others. He started telling me what a good friend I was and how my friendship was very important. The conversation migrated to how I could prove that I was his friend. I could prove it by allowing him to hug me from behind. I found out later that this was commonly known as corn-holing. He started removing my pants, which kicked in my survival instincts. I screamed for him to stop, which he refused. I kicked loose from his grasp, turned around, and noticed he had his pants down. I ran. He yelled that I was not his friend as I made my way back to my division.

I never told anyone about this experience. We never told! Thanks to the rumor mill at the home, this experience became well known. The enforcer came visiting. He was very angry. He yelled at me, letting me know in no uncertain terms that this predator was not my friend. He ordered me never to talk to older boys again. If his strategy was to scare me, it worked. Unfortunately, I overreacted. I decided not to make any friends at all. Some of the children in my division remarked that I was not playing with them, going to Town Hall to play basketball, and so on. For the rest of my stay at the home, I never had a normal interaction with the other children.

Extreme efforts were made to make sure all children experienced a memorable summer. Vacations were arranged with approved volunteer families. Those not on vacation could spend a week or two at the home camp grounds, go on excursions such as theme parks, or enjoy games in the woods surrounding the home. I enjoyed camp so much that I made it known to the staff that I would rather stay at the home during summer and attend camp.

One summer, three of us had no vacation and no summer camp. It was decided we would enjoy going to camp with the older boys. Surely the plan was for the older boys to make sure we had a good time. Each of us was assigned to one of the three barracks at the camp. Each barrack held about twelve children. I was comfortable being in the second barrack because I trusted Jack, one of that barrack's occupants. He must have been assigned, or had assumed, the responsibility of seeing to it I had a good time. After getting settled in, Jack took me to another barrack to see Benjamin. He was one of the three of us with no vacation, and a good friend.

The barrack was nearly empty, with only three or four children. What I saw when I entered that barrack caused nightmares for many years. Benjamin was on the top bunk with the predator. Upon seeing us, the predator covered himself and Benjamin with a sheet. Benjamin whimpered loudly. I heard the predator tell the other boys in the barrack that he would be finished in a minute and that they should try it. They all said something to the effect he was sick, but none of them tried to stop the predator. He was a big kid. One of the boys prevented my attempt to get on the top bed of the bunk, probably for my own good. I yelled out to Benjamin, asking if he was okay. He managed a whimper. I grabbed a baseball bat nearby, climbed up to the top bunk and held it above the predator's head, getting up enough nerve to bash his head in. Jack yelled to the predator that he better let Benjamin go unless he wanted his head bashed in. The predator looked from out of the sheet, saw the baseball bat, and complied. Benjamin jumped down from the bunk and ran out the back door of the barrack. I tried to follow, but Jack grabbed me and forced me towards the front door. It would be the last time I ever saw Benjamin. Some of the other boys in the barrack pleaded for me not to tell. They convinced Jack and I that they would look after Benjamin. I must have convinced myself that he would be okay. I realize now that was just wishful thinking.

I stayed very close to Jack, trying to get a glimpse of Benjamin, as if sight of him would mean he was okay. Jack was a trooper and tolerated my constant need to stay by his side. Later, he advised me that him and his friends were going to play a grown-up game. Despite my pleas to go with him, he insisted that I could not. He had a slingshot, so I surmised he was making sure I would not get hurt.

After Jack left, I hid underneath a bunkbed in the front corner of the barrack. Instinct told me that hiding in a corner with no escape was not a good idea. I sought a way to escape. I discovered that the floor of the barracks was about two foot short of the walls. The terrain in that area was very soft sand, easy to dig. I proceeded to dig an escape hole. About halfway done, I heard boys in the back of the barrack. One of them called out, "He has to be in here." Urgency and fear quickly became close companions. Despite the pain and blood from my fingers, the hole was quickly finished. One of the boys entered the barrack, saying, "We just want to talk to you." In hindsight, their aim had been just that, probably to make sure I would not snitch. As a matter of fact, two of these were good friends. However, considering what I saw, there was no way I was going to trust anyone from that bunk.

I escaped through the hole. I made my way along a dirt path behind the barracks, to the back door of the cabin where the counselors stayed. A light knock followed with a soft, "Help me!", brought no response, as did pounding and yelling. Realizing the chasers must have heard those cries for help, I joined the bushes below the river bank. Unfortunately, small critters we call chiggers had claimed those bushes. However painful the bites from those small critters were, pain is not pain when expectations are far worse. I very carefully slid down into the river, making sure to not make a splash. The river bottom behind the cabin was full of what appeared to be leaves and mud. I discovered that one had to grab ahold of these to stay underwater and out of sight. Drowning must have been a more attractive option than being caught. I stayed underwater much longer than normal. Upon surfacing and gulping for air, I was relieved the chasers were elsewhere. The two options were to cross the river into the woods and hide, or cross over to the other side and run for the dining hall. The dining hall was the better option, as certainly cooks or perhaps counsellors would be there.

I crawled out of the river and ran towards the dining hall. Just before reaching the dining hall, a boy appeared between me and the dining room. He managed to tear my t-shirt as I dodged him. I ran to the back of the dining hall, encountering a shower enclosure. Strangely enough, I do not remember screaming during this time. The shower enclosure was certainly no place to hide, as the entrance was also the only exit. Against all reasoning, I found myself in the shower. In hindsight, this was a very good strategy, one I must have learned when playing fox and hound. The hounds would not look in the obvious places, knowing the fox was too smart to hide there. Considerable relief was had as the chaser ran by the showers towards the river. As I exited the shower enclosure, he saw me. Back towards the kitchen and dining hall we went. It surely would have been easy to get to the dining hall, but terror must have affected my rationale. I opted for the bridge into the woods. Running towards the bridge, two other boys joined in, still yelling that they only wanted to talk to me.

Somehow I made it over the bridge, into the woods, and up a steep hill without being caught. They were right behind me. I ran along a well-beaten path on a hill above the river. I felt this cold chill all over my body. I started to cry, probably realizing the futility of outrunning these older boys. What happened next has me still wondering after all these years. It was as if my Guardian Angel swooped down and advised me to leave the beaten path and run through the woods. Though against my sense of reasoning, I obliged. After a few seconds of running through the woods, I got this very short-lived sensation "Hey, I'm running through the woods, my favorite game."

I seemed to have honed a talent that the chasers lacked. I was keenly aware they were falling behind. I encountered a tree that had long seen its end. Part of its bark had rotted, a sign that it could give way if one stepped on it. I ran very fast towards the log, stepping very lightly on the log as I jumped over. One of the chasers followed. Sounds of cussing and screaming in pain confirmed he had failed to step lightly. I encountered a dry gully and ran down at full speed without falling, a feat not accomplished by a chaser.

I encountered another gully. This one was very popular because we would swing over using a rope tied to a nearby tree. I was well familiar with this type of gully because of some very bad experiences trying to traverse similar ones when playing my favorite game. These gullies held overflow from the river. Once the water receded and the gullies were covered with leaves, they appeared to be quite innocent. In fact, the lower parts of the sides were deep mud, enough to get stuck in momentarily.

To successfully traverse such a gully, one would have to make a very good guess how far down the gully one could run before encountering that mud, then jump to the other side, hopefully landing above the mud line. Somehow, I knew where the mud started and ended. I successfully jumped to the other side. I heard a "squouch" sound, followed with the same response as the chaser stepping not so lightly on the log.

One of the other chasers had managed the gulley. I ran towards the tree with the rope. Luck or fate was on my side. It was tied to a limb on that side of the gully. In one motion, the rope was untied, and I swung to the other side. Once on the other side, the rope was wrapped around a bush, to prevent the chaser from using it. I continued running through the woods, now back towards the camp. Again, I heard some chasers yelling that they only wanted to talk to me. They certainly wanted to convince me not to snitch. By now, that is what I wanted to believe, but my instinct felt otherwise.

I came upon a group of bushes. They had very big thorns. Believing the chasers would not dare challenge these bushes, I crawled to the center, being careful not to scream from those very big and painful thorns. One of the chasers must have seen me. He ran directly into the bushes after me. It was a painful lesson on how those bushes survived in harsh environments. I panicked and ran out of those bushes, encountering another chaser who had given up and was making his way back to the camp. He turned around, and we again found ourselves running along a beaten path. It was the same one that my guardian angel previously advised me to abandon.

My strength was now drained. It was time to give up. My guardian angel, or myself, I know not which, decided there was one last chance. Two identical trees had grown on opposite sides of this beaten path, on top of a high cliff overlooking the river. A rope was tied to a limb overlooking the cliff, on the tree next to the cliff. It was used only by the bravest to swing out over the cliff, usually because of a dare, double dare. Losing grip of that rope would invite the grim reaper. Directly below was the Bass Hole, so named because it was home to a large bass that we could always see but never catch. Significant parts of the riverbed had dried up that year, consequences of a very hot summer with very little rain. The Bass Hole still had water, but there was dry river bed on both sides.

I slowed down, just enough to allow the chaser to catch up as I came upon the twin trees. I stopped in my tracks, falling to my knees, a stunt used to convince bullies not to give chase. While the bullies went flying over, sometimes injuring themselves, the chaser ended up on my back. While my intention was certainly not to use that rope, I grabbed ahold of it and stepped over the cliff. I could not hold on to the rope with him on my back, and we found ourselves free falling down the cliff. I folded my legs into my body and kicked him away from me. He went towards the sandy side of the cliff, and I went further out over the cliff, straight down.

The sensation of free falling, combined with the realization my ordeal would soon be over, is indescribable. Surely the fear of death would overcome all other fears. I did not experience such a fear! I felt very relaxed and glad that my ordeal would soon end. I landed on my side in the Bass Hole. I suffered from that impact for several years. That suffering would not be experienced if I had landed on the dry riverbed next to the Bass Hole. The impact sent the water and the bass out of is home, leaving me alone on the river bottom. I started feeling all over my body, checking myself for injuries. The shock of still being with the living was soon interrupted by the realization that I may not soon be. The water was now making its way back into the bass hole. I crawled out and discovered the bass on the bank, flipping over and over. Hey, I caught the bass! I tossed it back in its hole. No one would believe I caught it anyway. I glanced back and saw a lone chaser making his way down the sandy cliff towards the river. I did not see the other chasers.

It was all but one down and one to go. I made my way through bushes alongside the river and found myself next to the only road leading to and out of the camp. There were three options to escape. One was the long way, across an open field where plenty of bushes could provide cover. Another was shorter and certainly the best, as it led into the campgrounds. The third was still shorter, along the road leading away from the camp. There was a bend in that road, around which I could disappear. Success depended upon reaching these areas before the chaser emerged from the bushes next to the river. Quickness of feet was not an attribute I possessed. Normally, I would take the shortest route; toward the bend in the road away from camp. Again, my Guardian Angel intervened. The longer route across the field was highly recommended. Against my better judgement, I followed that recommendation. I just made it across the field before the chaser appeared from the bushes. I dove behind a tree. The chaser appeared from the bushes. I saw him look towards the camp, then towards the bend in the road. He never even considered I would try to make it across the field. The Guardian Angel's strategy worked! The chaser made his way towards the camp, searching the bushes lining the road.

I made my way through the woods on the other side of the camp and crawled under a bush next to the campgrounds. I looked out over the campground for that child I now believed was my Guardian Angel. I was bleeding from the effects of those thorns, my ankle was sprained, I was bruised up from the many falls in the woods, and my arm, shoulder, and back were in pain from landing in the bass hole. Fortunately, I was familiar with these pains from the woods game. As if to add insult to injury, salt from my sweat entered the scratches made by the wounds from those thorns. Again, pain is not pain when expectations are much worse. A snake appeared near my feet, making a hissing noise. It had fangs and put them to good use, striking me twice on my wet tennis shoes. Normally, I would have run. I was terrified of snakes. With more pressing concerns, its efforts were ignored. The snake finally slithered away, probably discouraged that its best was not good enough.

That which I sought finally appeared. I limped out of the bush, hurdled an iron fence, falling over with pain as my sprained ankle did not appreciate that effort. I limped through the large yard on the campgrounds and unsuccessfully attempted to jump over a ping pong table. I made it to Jack, grabbing onto his leg. Jack glanced down at me, noticed my condition, and asked, "What happened to you." I said nothing, hanging on to his leg for dear life.

Jack quickly surmised that other children were the problem. He yelled that if anyone messed with me, they would have to deal with him. Now, such warnings were seldom, if ever, offered. They would certainly be answered by those who lived for such opportunities. Most children saw my condition and offered to help me rather than meet Jack's challenge. Some other children were more interested in kicking Jack's butt for no other reason than that they wanted to kick his butt. They lined up. A voice came out from nowhere, "A fight! Great!" Andrew was a good friend of Jack's and seemed to believe in that trait we homies treasured: loyalty. Jack and Andrew made a rule that a challenger would first fight me. If they were successful, they had to fight Jack, and then if successful, Andrew. I did not appreciate them including myself in that challenge. Andrew explained I had to learn to take care of myself. The children in line disappeared. Some of them took me aside and gave me lessons in fighting. They explained that Jack and Andrew would not be around, all of the time. For the rest of camp, I never left Jack's sight. At times, Jack ordered me to stay in a play room adjacent to the dining hall, as they were going to play some rough games. Although I agreed, I kept him well in sight.

23

The Best of Times

cannot remember the rest of the time at camp. My only objective was to keep near my Guardian Angel. Camp was over. It was time to return to the home. While only disappointing for most of the children, it was terrifying for me. This meant dealing with the predator. Running away was the only option. As all were getting ready to leave, I made my way down the road exiting the camp. Sort of a sad attempt at sneaking away. When I was sure the camp staff did not notice me, I started running. I had taken no more than a couple of steps when a car appeared, making its way towards the camp. It was too late to hide. I waved at the people in the car. Sort of a sad attempt to make them believe I was simply hanging out halfway out of the campgrounds. The car went by and started towards the camp. Just as I thought it was safe to continue my escape, someone in the car yelled, "That's him, look at the picture." A lady got out of the car and asked my name. They had a picture of me. A non-truth would have been futile. I told the truth. The lady said I was going on vacation with them. She explained they had all my clothes, and would be taken directly to their farm. My immediate thought was I would not have to go back to the home and you know who. Three meals with a family certainly influenced my decision to go with them. I got into the car.

This vacation was one of the turning points in my life. Very poor farmers and their three children with very rich hearts took me into their fold. They treated me as one of their own. Anxious to become a part of the family, I volunteered help with all that the other children had to do. My experiences with this family could be another story. Suffice it to say that my life took a turn for the best because of them.

I always dreamed about once again being part of a family. We were a family at the home, but that life was very different than one with parents. This vacation allowed me to experience that family life I wanted. There was a huge difference between home life and the life with this family. Most startling was living with girls. At the home, the only time spent with girls were scheduled and well-monitored activities. Living with them allowed me insight to their trials and tribulations. The mother payed attention to me, and like a parent punished me as she did her own children. No longer was I a pebble on the beach. I thought I was a significant part of the family. The mother, and sometimes the children, were willing to listen. At the home, chores were viewed as work. On this vacation, chores were viewed as work necessary to support a family. I worked twice as hard on this vacation than I ever did at the home, and enjoyed it. Suffice it to say that this vacation made me aware of the differences between life with parents and life in the home. At the end of the summer I had realized what all homies dream about; to be part of a family. When it was time for me to return to the home, I cried. The mother convinced the home to allow me to stay longer. This was repeated twice more, allowing me to be part of their family right up to the day school started. Finally, I had to return.

I could not handle the stark difference in life in the home and as part of a family. I cried quietly under my blanket at night, yearning for that which was not possible. I wrote a letter to the family, explaining it was too difficult for me to return to the home after being with them. The home read all letters sent to and out of the home. They censored portions of each letter they decided should not be read. The enforcer revealed this to me and retrieved a letter I had written to that wonderful vacation family. So many words were blacked out that it was decided not to send it. It occurred to me that this family had never found out my reasons for not wanting to go on vacation with them again. They probably thought I never appreciated the vacation!

I was extremely bothered about this. I decided to visit this family before returning to college that spring. The intent was to make sure they knew how much I appreciated their kindness. I hitched a ride to Anderson. I had an idea of how to get to their farm from the times we rode bikes into Anderson. It took some time, but I walked to their farm. It was exciting to realize I could explain to them how I felt. The old hog barn was still there, with a semi-circle driveway, and a wonderful, old farm house. As I was about to manage the fence blocking the driveway, one of the girls in the family came out of the house, followed with a small girl that I recognized as one of my homies. This family was doing what they did best, giving a child the experience of a family. I watched them for several minutes. I never revealed my presence. As I was making my way back to Anderson, I felt a sense of goodness, knowing they still sponsored a child.

At the end of the vacation, I had to return to the home. In my mind, it meant encountering the predator. I decided to go back to the home and then take off at the first opportunity.

24

Back Home

While the enforcer was taking me back to Division 17, I inquired about the predator. He informed me that this troubled child would no longer bother anyone in the home. My relief was indescribable. I took this to mean the predator was no longer at the home. I would not have to run away! I cried, which was the first time I realized that both ecstasy and terror can cause the same emotional response.

SURVEYING

Upon entering Division 17, I found myself taking a survey of what children I would have to live with the next year. Of primary concern were bullies and children who were just mean. Noticeably, all the children surveyed were those I trusted to a fault. The two no-nonsense kids were there, very good friends. Another was one I spent many hours passing the time away as school janitors. One was kind to a fault, and one you could easily convince to release some pop and popcorn. Another was the same child reading one of the popular literary works, and described the book at a level to this day I do not understand. Another had an appreciation for the martial arts and was anxious to teach others his expertise. He used this expertise to convince his own brother to stop using some of us as his punching bag. Another child was very tough but a friend. He made sure his brother, a bully, also did not use us as his punching bag. Another child was one who valued loyalty above all other characteristics and one whose sisters were certainly the object of many fantasies. Another was a tall child who would become a star baseball pitcher. Another was the same child I had tried to mimic, to gain attention while a toddler. He thought he was the coolest kid in school. Many of the young ladies seemed to agree. Another was very big, very tough, who did not invite trouble but never ran away from it either. As tough as he seemed, we others were amused when he fainted from the sight of blood. He once hit a baseball so far that the opposite team stood and cheered. Another was a master lock picker who was instrumental in regaining our stolen possessions. Another was one that I had a great deal of admiration. He wanted to be involved in whatever was going on. He could not make the basketball team and could not be a ball boy. He never stopped there. He tried out and made the cheerleading team, something that was extremely rare in this era. We won the junior-high tourney as he and the girls led the cheering. I made it a point to give him the trophy; however, his shyness prevented that. I believe many of us on the team gave another one hundred percent attempting to match his spirit. Another was a former Division 11 boy that we always played with during the time in Division 9. He now lived with the rest of us, complements of the Supreme Court. My only complaint was that he always beat me to the old steam registers in the winter mornings, upon which one could lay and enjoy the heat. He was destined to be a track star. Another was the smartest of all of us, who was referred to as the matter-of-fact kid, as what he said seemed to be just that. I could go on, but the bottom line is they were all trustworthy friends. I decided to stay at the home with these friends.

ALMOST RUNNING AWAY

I was ecstatic about finding myself with friends I trusted. We talked consistently and laughed out loud as we described our summer vacations. Our governess did not share our excitement. She gave an order to cease and desist. We failed to recognize that order as the one interpreted as, "We will die a painful death if we do not obey." Once back at the division, she chose the one talking the loudest to punish. She gave me, and only me, one week on the punishment chair! An unfortunate way of life was for all to be punished by the bad behavior of a few. While this is not different than children of other families, the sheer number of children living together ensured this would be far more common. Respect for that rule of rules inadvertently helped propagate this fate. Those children that were man enough to "Man Up", and admit to an infraction, earned the approval of their peers. Those that did not own up suffered what children fear the most.

There were three types of punishment commonly used. The most common punishment was time on the punishment chair. It was no stranger to all. It was always near the door of the divisions, surely to make sure all those coming and going could see the poor unfortunate. The next most used punishment was demerits. This also was no stranger to all. The home paid the children to perform their daily chores and to work in trade shops. The pay was just enough to get some popcorn, candy and pop at Town Hall, the activity center at the home. A portion or all this pay was not forthcoming for children that misbehaved. This explained the destitute status of many while at the home.

The least used form of punishment was spanking. Spanking was state-sanctioned. The state implemented a very good, formal system for spanking. Reviews by several were made to determine if spankings were appropriate and necessary. Records were kept to document those spankings. At the expense of objections from my homies, and those viewing spankings as abuse, it is fair to say those that received formal spankings deserved them.

Though surely not sanctioned by the state, threats to be spanked, or worse, were used. Because of that rules of rules, or the fear of retributions, these would go undiscovered by those that could prevent them. Some children held their torments from this abuse inside and let it fester for years. It could affect their lives for a very long time. Although rare, some fought back physically from their abusers. Some would be forced to leave because of this. One should realize that children outside the home have that deterrent most effective for preventing abuse and retaliation; love. Respect was the main deterrent for children and staff in the home. It was much less effective than love.

While time on the punishment chair was not a big deal; being singled out was seen as an injustice. My behavior in this respect was very strange. My life at the home was very good. However, I had been beat by bullies, attacked by a sexual predator, scorned by a girl that believed life as a nun was preferable to being my girl friend, and many other bad incidents. Of all of these, the injustice of being singled out for punishment turned out to be the line in the sand. I cried.

Most children are blessed by those who are willing to listen and kiss away their tears. Except for those rare visits by loved ones, the tears from the home children could only disappear through their own efforts. Sometimes their tears disappeared through the comforts offered by other children. On rare occasions the home staff were willing to sympathize. Though a sympathetic and caring staff, too much sympathy or attention to a specific child was dangerous. Many a home staff would leave because of their fondness for a specific child, and the realization they were helpless to kiss away their tears. Without those to kiss away their tears, it is entirely possible serious problems of the children were internalized. They certainly resurfaced later, some after many years, affecting the lives of the children again and again. I was blessed with two children I referred to as the no-nonsense kids. When I sought their advice they always told me what was necessary. Unfortunately, what was necessary and what was needed sometimes collided. What was necessary was to "Man Up!". What was needed, someone to kiss away those tears.

Outraged at the injustice, I left the punishment chair and encountered the enforcer at Town Hall. The room was filled with my peers. A request to talk with him alone was refused. He never gave me a chance to plead my case. He yelled at me to stop acting like a baby and take my punishment like a man. This must have been extremely upsetting. I cried in front of my peers. The other children were whispering to each other, and some were laughing. It was the lowest point of my life in the home. An exception may be the time when I had to learn the ones and twos of going to the bathroom. The enforcer realized how low I felt. Later, I heard him arguing with my governess. He told her to keep an eye on me as it was entirely possible I would run away. She laughed, and told him that he was overreacting. After those many years, with so many children, the enforcer could accurately predict outcomes. His concern was right on target. One of my siblings informed me that for about a week, the enforcer came into our dormitory and checked to make sure I was in bed and not elsewhere. Running away seemed to be a common thread among the children.

Home life was a challenge for all children. It was hard for some children to truly understand the love of the home. This love manifested itself as three good meals a day, the camaraderie of virtual siblings, wonderful governesses, security, education, and opportunities. Those who consciously or unconsciously realized this love adapted quickly to home life. Those that could not adapt met other fates. Some that could not adapt, yet realized the home was their only option, were forced to a life of misery in the home. Some misbehaved so much they were removed, or ran away.

The love of the home served well as the prison walls for those that disliked their situation at the home. Those who dared run away enjoyed sort of a hero status to many. Perhaps we recognized they had the guts to do what most of us only thought about. It is common at homecomings to hear children brag about running away.

One of my friends bragged, "I ran away twenty-three times."

Being my annoying self, I responded, "Yes, but you ended up back in the home all twenty-three times!"

He laughed, saying "That I did."

It did not take long for most children to adapt to home life. I believe that when they did, the home was their best option. Most problems thereafter seemed to be those than any child would experience. There were situations for a child when running away was the preferable option. Being singled out for punishment was such a situation for myself.

I possessed the very bad habit of carefully planning exploits, and taking advantage of whatever opportunities were presented. An opportunity presented itself that allowed me to do just what the enforcer feared. The home planned a day when children could spend the entire day doing whatever. The only requirement was attendance at breakfast and supper. The whatever contemplated was to be far away from perceived injustice, before they discovered I was missing.

I tried to break into a place that stored just about everything. Appropriately, it was called the Storeroom. The security of this building was outstanding. The walls were all brick with no windows. Every night the doors were locked with dead locks and huge chains with heavy duty locks placed around the handles of the double doors. Attempts to bribe a friend with the expertise to pick those locks failed. I guess he had a line in the sand over which he never crossed. I had to depend on stealth and deception. The day before we were to experience considerable freedom, I went to the Storeroom under the pretense of getting some cooking pans needed by the cooks. The manager let me in and told me what I wanted was upstairs. All I had to do was to sign an inventory sheet. I went upstairs and signed the sheets. Instead of exiting, I hid out in the store room behind what appeared to be very old road signs. Near the end of the day, the store room was closed and locked. I retrieved an old army tent, matches, an old army water canister, and, of all things, a baseball bat. I have no idea why the bat, although I did like playing baseball! Upon attempting to leave with the loot, I discovered the extent of my stupidity. It was impossible to manage the lock and chains on the outside handles. Breaking into the store room was impossible. Breaking out was even more impossible. With the prospect of spending the night in the store room, a strategy was contemplated to explain where I was for the entire night. Just as I had decided on one, a strange sound was heard at the back door. It was the backup warning of a huge truck backing up to the loading docks. About a half hour later, the store manager appeared with several older boys. He unlocked the door, and they commenced to unload the truck. When I believed they were all inside the store. I darted out the door with the loot. One of the older boys was by the truck. He looked at me momentarily, then quickly motioned for me to run. I thanked him and stuffed the items under some bushes across the street, next to the lake.

Later that evening I broke into the kitchen, if you can call opening a door that was never locked breaking in. I appropriated a box of cereal and some other food items. I added these to the other items in the bushes. After everyone had retired for the night, these items were moved next to a huge group of steps leading up to the administration building. They were on the outskirts of the home grounds, on the path to the woods: my escape route.

As I made my way back to the division, I encountered two of the home staff. They were holding hands and laughing like school children as they ran out of the administration building. That they were surprised to see me so late at night, or even at all, would be an understatement. The man asked why I was out so late at night. It was as if this question silently bounced off me and right back to them. He quickly realized the predicaments we shared. He added he would not tell anyone if I would not tell anyone I agreed. At that time my thought was "Who cares"? On hindsight, it was funny.

It was the day when we only had to be present at breakfast and supper. Right after breakfast, I made my getaway. I retrieved the items borrowed from the store room and kitchen. It did not take long to discover why those who enjoy the wild travel light. I ditched all but the water canister and a small amount of the cereal. A slow runner I was, but run all day I could. After a few hours, I happened by an old farm house with an apple orchard and a huge barn.

While gathering some apples, the aroma of a fresh apple pie got my attention. It reminded me of the apple pies my grandma Mitchell made. As Grandma did, the pies hot out of the oven were placed in an open window to cool off. As I did with Grandma's pies (sorry Grandma), I commenced to test their hotness by sticking my finger in them. I had learned the hard way to never set your teeth into an apple pie right out of the oven. While testing a pie, I heard a dog snarling near my feet. It was a very big and very ugly, dog. It wagged its tail slowly, which told me that bodily harm was not the intention. I took a pie that tested okay. The dog stopped snarling and wagged its tail very fast. It dawned on me that the dog was not snarling at me for taking the pie. He was warning me he had better get a piece! The dog, I, and the pie made our way to the back of the huge barn. Just as we were about to make short work of that pie, the dog quickly took off with its tail between its legs. I glanced over to the side of the barn. A farmer was glaring at me.

After the usual lecture about taking what was not mine, the farmer looked at me intently. He then asked if I was from the home. The farmers living near the home had probably been alerted to children running away. After admitting I was, he invited me into his home, bribing me with something to eat. He and his wife convinced me to return to the home. The farmer left to call the home. I thought about taking off while he was gone, but the smell of fresh biscuits convinced me otherwise.

His wife commenced to warm up some baked potatoes, probably from one of the farmer's fields nearby. She removed some pheasant from the refrigerator, probably shot the day before, and put it in an oven with the potatoes to heat up. She started boiling some sweet corn, probably from their own crops. She then uncovered those biscuits, probably made that morning. She buttered them, probably made from the cream rising to the top of those old milk cans. She gave me a glass of milk, probably from milking the cows that morning. She proceeded to make some mashed potatoes using a strategy I employ to this day. She broke open the baked potatoes, crushed the insides, smothered them with real butter, poured some milk on them, and mixed them with a fork. It was as if we had fast forwarded to thanksgiving in heaven.

As I was finishing this feast, the farmer returned. He explained that a lady at the home told him they had not discovered that I was missing. If I magically showed up before supper, no one would be the wiser. The farmer drove me back to the home and dropped me off. I did not tell my buddies about this, knowing the ribbing I would get. The home staff knew about this futile attempt. After all, rumors know no boundaries.

While doing my chores, I had to visit the storeroom, from which I had appropriated the tent and other items. Each time I visited, the storeroom manager made it a point to tell me that someone had stolen a tent from storage. They found it below the steps leading to the administration building. He added that there were many expensive items in the storeroom, but the thief chose to take only a tent. He then asked me, every time I saw him, if I knew anything about that. I knew that he knew, he knew that I knew, and we both knew that the other knew that we knew. I never bothered to say anything, and he always laughed after asking that question. I saw the farmer and his wife several times at basketball games. We waved at each other: mine a signal of appreciation, and theirs a, "You are welcome."

SOMEONE TO TALK TO

A child needs someone to talk to; one that has experienced the trials of growing; one that has made mistakes and suffered the consequences. Such are the responsibilities of parents. When these parents cannot, or should not, act in this mode, a child is left with their problems, and worse consequences than these problems alone can create. Unless, other adults volunteer their time and their hearts. Such circumstances were common of home children. Some children could talk to their parents or relatives on rare visits. Some children could depend upon a governess or a teacher in times of need. However, the need was many. Those that could give advice were few. Consequently, most children were left to their own means to deal with problems. The fortunate ones had the tools to be successful. Many of the unfortunate ones did not. Perhaps that was best. When children left the home, they would be, for the most part, on their own. They had to learn how to deal with their own problems much quicker than children with parents.

For ten years, I was one of those unfortunate ones. I had always wanted to run away, with expectations the consequences of ignoring those problems would disappeared. Other expectations made me a prisoner of my own volition; such as the love of the home; loving comrades, three meals a day, schooling, and many other forms of love. Problems left unattended grow within. They soon run out of space. It is this time that I was, in the words of those westerners, at the end of my rope. A decision was made when I found myself crying at night, seemingly for no reason. I planned to run away. I was sitting on an iron rail fence in the back of our high school, near the track. It was just after supper, and there would be enough time to be far away by the time anyone noticed I was missing. A young adult lady walked down the path by the fence. I waved hi. She approached. She knew my name. She asked if I could walk with her. She explained that she had fainting spells. Her doctor told her to make sure someone was with her while she walked.

We walked down a path across from the older boys' divisions, along the baseball field. I engaged in a conversation. I asked her if she was just getting exercise? She said she was, but at her doctor's instructions. I never asked why. She asked how I was doing. I responded with the standard untruthful answer. She must have detected that untruthfulness. She stated that it must be difficult living in a home with no parents. I gave another untruthful, standard answer. I said it was not bad at all. My lack of sincerity got her attention. She stopped in her tracks and looked at me intently. She smiled, as if to let me know my lie was understandable. She told me that all children need an adult to talk to; one with whom they can discuss problems. We continued our walk. I mentioned there were a few problems, but there was no one to talk to about them. She stopped again, and told me that if I wanted to discuss them with her, she would listen. By this time, we were back near the track. We sat in the bleachers. I told her of some problems. Interesting enough, she offered no solutions. On hindsight, I believe she was simply trying to get me to understand why I was having those problems. She had never experienced life in the home. It would be difficult for her to offer solutions. After talking for a while, she told me that she walked at the same time every day. If I wanted to walk with her, I could. Every day, at the same time, she appeared, only with a friend. When I wanted to talk about a problem, I went with them. After several weeks, she asked if our talks were helping.

After thinking about that, I realized that those problems seemed to have disappeared! I told her that. She smiled, then said that we may not be able to walk together much longer, but I could talk to her if I really needed to. For the next few weeks I sat on the rail fence, waiting for her. I waved and she waved back. As time went by, she skipped days. I noticed that she seemed to hold on to her friend more and more. Finally, her walks were no more.

I asked several home staff about her. They all had no idea who she was. I doubted their sincerity of that. One simply cannot walk in clear view of everyone without being noticed. Be that as it may, I could not find anyone that would give me information about her. I gave up. I owed her so much, and wanted to thank her. It appeared that I would never be able to do this.

My life in the home improved. I could not forget what she had done for me. Sometimes I went out and sat on that iron rail fence near the track, and visualized her walking down the path. It gave me a good feeling. It was a Sunday. I had skipped church, and was leaning on a fence near Lake Graham, right across form the home garage. Our home bus returned from Knightstown. Every Sunday they took the Catholics to a nearby town for church. I waved to the driver. He was very young. He parked the buss, and came over to the fence. I had heard that his young wife had passed away. I expressed my condolences. He revealed to me that before she died, she requested to see me. He had no idea why, and no idea that we even knew each other. Regardless, he asked the home staff if I could visit her. The home staff decided to not allow that, for reasons that still are a mystery today. When he told his wife that, she told him to tell me that she enjoyed the walks. I returned to the iron rail fence, and cried.

25

Band Memories

While working at the home in the summer, my former track coach and I were assigned to sand and varnish the band room floor at Morton Memorial High School. He was now seventy plus years old. I asked why he continued to work at such an age. Apparently, for the thirty plus years before, teachers at Morton Memorial were paid the lowest wages possible. That year the state saw the error in this. They made a policy to pay teachers the highest wages in the county. This track coach indicated that he was being paid so much, he could not afford to retire; if that makes sense. To my surprise, this seventy-plus track coach decided to try out all the instruments in the band room. I had to get in on that. Our duet played some of the God-awful music of all time, but we had a lot of fun. This reminded me of the fun as a member of the band at Morton Memorial High School.

Morton Memorial was a very, very small school, with only about eighty-five students in high school. It was imperative that a high percentage participate in athletics and the marching band. Participation in the marching band was most important for boys as it was a boy-only activity. The sole exception while I was in the home was when a very good baton twirler insisted she lead the band. She was so pretty and talented that no one questioned her. We envied the trombone players. They were at the front of the band. Later the band became a boy and girl affair, appropriately so. The band director confessed that girls should have been in the band long ago. Many were much better than the boys. He had only two complaints. One was that he no longer could give the marchers a swift kick in the butt if they did not keep up marching. The other was that he could no longer tell those boys-only jokes.

In the early 50s, it was common for Morton Memorial's marching band to place near the top ten of marching bands at the state fair. It was an amazing feat considering we had only one hundred and fifty in high school. Our band director took his job seriously and saw fit that we did too. Because he was old school and a war veteran, we found ourselves marching to a lot of Susa's marches. We also experienced swift kicks in the butt when we did not keep up with the others while marching. He spent so much time in Germany protecting our freedoms that he was fluent in their language. We found ourselves marching to that cadence of eins (ighnss), zwei (tsvigh), drei (drigh), view (feer). If we did not keep up during a march, we heard those all-too-familiar words "mach schnell", which meant in German, "shake a leg". To us it had an additional meaning: keep up or get your butt kicked. We loved this man. Unlike many others, he did not show pity. He expected us to give all we could and contribute to the success of the band. When we did not, a reminder was forthcoming. There was one experience when Charles and I were the benefactors of a reminder.

NONSENSE AND SENSE

Band members were responsible for the conditions of their instruments and uniforms. In terms we believed were the difference between life and death, the band director convinced us that our uniforms and instruments must show up for an event in perfect condition. His favorite phrase was, "Show up with your instruments and uniforms in less than perfect condition, and I will kick your butt from here to Berlin," illustrating his involvement with the war.

Charles and I were late getting our uniforms from the cleaners. We were also late getting to the band room. It was pouring with a capital P. We had to make it to the band room on time, with the uniforms in perfect condition. In this case, it meant not wet. It would be impossible to be there on time, and much less impossible to keep the uniforms dry. About two hundred yards of open field separated us and the band room at the school. I recommended we had better run to get there on time. Charles submitted it was more important to get the uniforms there as dry as possible. He submitted that it would be better to walk, rather than run. His reasoning was as follows. If we ran, we would get the uniforms wetter, as we would be running thru the raindrops. If we walked, less raindrops would fall on them. What? Where are the two no-nonsense kids when you need them? I thought Charles's rationale made sense! We walked in the downpour of downpours from Division 29 to the band room at the school. Once inside the school, we looked at each other and started laughing. Water was running, not dripping, from our clothes and from the uniforms we were supposed to protect.

We made our way to the band room, trying to avoid you know who. Unfortunately, we encountered you know who. Our explanations of why we were late fell on deaf ears as his interest was with those uniforms. He realized they were dripping wet. He got so mad you could see the blood rising from his neck to his forehead. He asked, "How in God's name did these uniforms get this wet?"

Charles started to explain; starting out with "Well we thought that ...." I stopped him and nodded my head in that universal language of "Don't." We stood in silence as the riot act was read to us. We would be shining all the instrument for next few weeks.

WHERE'S THE BATON?

One experience in the marching band gave me a phrase that I've used throughout my life to pick up my spirits. On that day of remembrance for our veterans' efforts, and to remember those that had fallen while in the home, the children assembled their band and color guard. As the band played that well-known refrain of Chopin, we all made our way to a cemetery. It was the final resting place for those that fell while in the home. Most were civil war veterans. There we stood in silence while Taps was played and echoed from the woods.

On that day of remembrance, our band director showed up with a package, and a smile from ear-to-ear. He got on his podium and held the package above his head as if it were his newborn child.

He said, "It's here. You will not believe how many asses I had to kick, and how many I had to kiss, to get this."

That certainly sparked our attention. The package held a long, wonderful, beautiful baton, with multiple-colored tallows and embedded jewels. Judging from our and the band director's reactions, the entire baton was solid gold.

He carefully handed it to our drum major, along with a warning, "Guard this with your life. If anything happens to this baton, I will kick your butt from here to Berlin."

He was dead serious, with a capital D and S. We went outside and lined up in our marching formation next to the high school, alongside several huge walnut trees. The signal was received for the band to march to the cemetery. The band director ordered the drum major to bring the band to attention. This was accomplished by swinging the baton in a vertical motion while simultaneously blowing a whistle. Hearing that whistle, we all stood to attention. Our eyes were focused on the drum major twirling that new baton. The quality control in manufacturing that baton must have been lacking. The centrifugal force from the circular motion forced the top of the baton with the tassels to separate from its body. It shot straight up and stuck in a branch high up in one of those walnut trees. The drum major found himself twirling the other half. He never saw the other half stick high in the tree. He desperately turned around and around, looking for the other half of the baton. We started laughing, ever so slightly. It was difficult to laugh hard, considering the somberness associated with this event. We were more concerned for our band leader. It would not be pretty what would happen when our band director discovered the missing baton. Unfortunately, he did. Like the band leader, he also never saw the baton stick in the tree. Him demeanor and voice told us all that we needed to be somewhere else.

He asked the drum major, "Where's the baton?"

The drum major made that universal signal of holding his arms open, signaling "I have no idea."

That scenario caused us to laugh so hard we were holding onto each other, almost in tears. There was not time to look for the baton, so the band director ordered the drum major to start the march without the baton. We proceeded to the resting place for those that saw their time end while in the home. In respect for the moment, we remained somber on the way there and during the service. As we returned, someone said, "Where's the baton?" We started laughing. I could not get that event out of my mind and laughed hard whenever it was recalled. Unfortunately, it was recalled each time I went to school, as I had to pass under that walnut tree. Now that I am in the twilight of my years, somber moments seem to come more and more. Appropriately so, as they certainly prepare me for what is to come.

To pick up my spirits, I simply say to myself, "Where's the Baton?".

DREAMS

Some dreams are visions of what could be. Attainment of these dreams is far less important than the efforts we make towards making them re-alities. Through these efforts, we learn the importance of dedication, hard work, and the boldness to forge ahead despite setbacks. Born in the 40s, I listened to the sounds of the big bands, complements of those old, classic AM radios. You oldsters are familiar with the type. They gave more static than music and continually required re-tuning to keep the station signal strong. If you tuned them at the extremes, you could hear pilots talking. Over time, the big band sounds were replaced by country and the beginnings of rock and roll. It was disap-pointing that the stations stopped playing my favorite music. To my liking, the big band music was preserved, complements of our band director and one of the home staff.

One of our home staff was once a member of a big band. An amazing player, we made it a point to corner him every Christmas and have him play with us. Our band director was a student of the big band. Like so many souls during that era, his dreams were interrupted, and perhaps shattered, by the war. These two created a small group of musicians molded after the big bands of the 30s and 40s. The band was named *The Mortonairres*. Among music popular in the 50s, they played those wonderful sounds of the 30s and 40s. As this band played the music I loved, my dream was to become part of this 40s-style big band. As only the best musicians were invited to try out, I practiced long and hard to realize my dream. The day of reckoning came. The band director visited our classroom and invited several of my friends to try out. While extremely disappointed about not being invited, I was not surprised. These friends were much better musicians. As if someone in charge of fates was sympathetic, a sequence of events came about that allowed a second opportunity to attain that dream I believed was unreachable.

During gym, one of the bigger boys was tripped. It was a retribution from an inadvertent slap. The gym teacher saw only the retribution and expelled me. He explained that it was for my own health, as these bigger boys were — much bigger. I dutifully reported to the principal's office during this gym hour. Whatever the reason, I was the only one who showed up.

After several days, I realized the principal was probably never notified of my expulsion. Being one not to waste such an opportunity, the halls of the school were visited, searching for whatever. It was that time during the school year when this 40s-style group practiced to play music for the annual dance recital. The dancers were very good, and their recital was without doubt the favorite school event of the year. I should have been sitting in the principal's office. Instead, I sat by the door right inside the hallway to the band room, out of sight of anyone happening by. There I listened to this group practice for the dance recital. To my liking, our band director could not help but occasionally play my favorite music.

One day, there was more silence than music. I had a strange sensation that someone was staring at me. I glanced up. There was the band director. He asked why I was not in class. I told him I was kicked out. He asked why I was sitting by the band room. I told him I liked listening to big band music. He asked me to name my favorite big band leader. I mentioned one very well known. He asked why that one was my favorite. I answered that this band leader played the same instrument I did in the marching band. He asked me to name my favorite songs of the big bands, which I did. He looked at me intently. I realized my newfound freedom would soon end. He then asked if I wanted to try out for the 40s-style band. I quickly answered yes. He told me to show up at practice the next day. I did, and was assigned to the third chair alto saxophone.

Now, seldom if ever is there a solo played by a musician other than first chair. However, the band director selected music with a solo played by, you probably guessed it, the third chair alto saxophone. I was unaware of this. When we reached the solo, I was somewhat concerned many had stopped playing, and more concerned that they were staring at me. One of our exceptional musicians sitting close by whispered to me that it was my solo. I had to stand up and play something, anything. This I did. However bad it was, and it was, I got through that ordeal. After the song was over, the band director took off his glasses and started wiping them. We in the marching band were familiar with this habit. It meant something was terribly wrong. Expectations to realize my dream took a nose dive.

He then said, "That was an interesting solo," which was the nice way of saying you know what.

Then he said, "But you know what? He never quit, he never quit. Welcome to the band."

I cried, laughed, then cried again, realizing the dream had become a reality. Eventually, the school office found out I had been kicked out of gym class and had not reported. After the usual lecture about getting along with others, I was sent back to gym. I apologized to the gym teacher for being a brat. He asked what I had done for the last few weeks. I told him I had listened to big band music. At first, it appeared he wanted to ask for a clarification. However, having been the recipient of some of my previous interesting clarifications, I believe he decided it was something he really did not want to know. To this day, my favorite music is from the 30s and 40s, and being in *The Mortonairres* is the only dream I ever attained.

DIXIE

Everyone needs to experience the satisfaction of doing something good in their life. Such was the case when our 40s-style band and the dance troupe entertained inmates in a mental hospital. It was hard to judge how or if our performances were appreciated. Some inmates were much like my friends when I start to speak: indifferent. Others were like my friends when I stopped speaking: unmistakably enthusiastic.

For several years, one of the inmates yelled out several times during our performances, "Play Dixie".

It was a request that could not be accommodated. This inmate never gave up. Each year we heard that same request. Finally the band director had us practice a song popular in the deep south. When we heard that desperate yell, we stopped playing, changed our music to one of the deep south, and obliged. The hospital's director told us the inmate cried, an emotion he previously had never exhibited.

LISTEN TO THE STARS

There were wonderful experiences playing in that 40s-style band. It was referred to as the dance band because it accompanied the dancers. The dance band and the dancers traveled to entertain several, wonderful organizations. One experience however was not so wonderful. It taught me that evil exists everywhere. This experience started at the tender age of eight years old, long before getting into the dance band. Our division was adjacent to Division 10; home for about fifteen girls, all the same color and of all ages. An angel ever so sweet caught my eye and fueled my imaginations, even at that age when I was supposed to hate girls. A hi was all I could offer, but it usually bought a smile. About a year later, these children were integrated with the other children. My angel left to the other side of the lake where the girls lived. Although gone from sight, she was still close to my heart. Years later, she was part of the dance troupe and I was part of the 40s-style band that played music to which they danced. She danced solo to that classic, Sweet Georgia Brown. I practiced long hours to memorize that song so I could catch a glimpse of her dancing rather than read the music.

We children took great pride in presenting a good show. This was especially true for organizations that sponsored events at the home. They made sure no child was forgotten and we wanted so much to give an unforgettable performance. We were invited to play for one such organization. I cannot recall which one.

We played, danced, and sang our best for these good Samaritans. It was time for my angel's performance, one surely to be a highlight. Our dance director instructed us to skip that song and her performance. I thought she was sick and asked one of her friends in the band if she was okay. He looked extremely bothered and said she was okay. It was the way he said this that led me to realize the reason we skipped that song and her dance was rooted in bigotry. I could not believe what was happening, especially from such wonderful people. I refused to play for the remainder of the performance. The band director was not pleased; however, he was understanding. He never punished me.

After the performance, we piled into the bus to go home. My angel sat alone, sad and gazing out the window. I stopped to say something but could not come up with any words. One of her friends said it would be best to leave her alone. I sat on the seat behind her. It was a very clear night. Twinkling stars entertained all looking their way. I recalled a song with a lesson about bigotry hidden within its lyrics. The lyrics revealed that there are many, many stars. Each star is different, of different sizes, and of different colors. Each has their own space in the universe. At any one time, each shine brighter than the others. I hoped my angel was listening to those stars.

Irony reveals itself in many, different ways. Later that year, our governess insisted we all watch TV. There was a very entertaining group playing that game Hoosiers claim their own. The Harlem Globe

Trotters entertained to that classic Sweet Georgia Brown. I am sure no one skipped their performance. I felt some tears upon my cheeks.

PROTESTING

Because of the way my angel was treated, I refused to participate in activities sponsored by organizations. I over reacted. Many wonderful members of various organizations sponsored a child in the home. They occasionally visited as a group, allowing the children to visit with their sponsor. Rather than meet with my sponsor, I and my transistor radio visited Sadie, a companion who kept me company during difficult times. Punishment was waiting when I returned, as I was required to visit with my sponsor.

After several similar instances of visiting Sadie rather than my sponsor, I was ordered to go see the enforcer. It would be the only time of my stay in the home that I had to do that! A man and woman were talking with the enforcer. The enforcer took me into the hallway and gave me a lecture about how sponsors took great pains to make sure each child was not forgotten. The least I could do was visit with them. He was right of course. However, I did not want to give an explanation about my protest. The man and woman introduced themselves. They indicated that they missed visiting with me. They handed me a present, mentioning they had heard I was a very good shortstop. I thought long and hard about taking that present. I never took it. The enforcer got mad. He again took me into the hallway and repeated the earlier lecture. He threw up his hands like he was giving up, then asked me point blank why I was acting so strange? I wanted to explain, but could not. The enforcer sensed there was a reason. He told me that his door was always open if I want to discuss it. The woman must have sensed there was a good reason. As I was leaving, she ran after me and convinced me to take the present. Later in life I explained to the enforcer about my small protest. He said that the home had no control over the actions of the sponsors.

26

Indifference

Indifference is an evil not easily cured. Its infestation affects the host for many years. It surely did for many home children. It was not until about my third year in college that I realized how much.

A newly-hired teacher at the home could not understand why no one in a class wanted to further their education after graduating from the home. He asked me to speak to them about how important this was. He explained that this class was exceptional. Many were more than capable of succeeding in college. As I talked with these children, I realized how indifferent they were to furthering their education. If they left the home with this attitude, it would be an opportunity missed; possibly one that would affect their futures. The best program implemented by the State was to pay tuition to the graduates from the home. It was an excellent opportunity. Unfortunately, the indifference of many children to furthering their education limited the effectiveness of the program.

I had a conversation with a about this indifference with a reveled member of the home staff at homecoming. He offered an interesting explanation. He explained that many children in the home never had mentors or loved ones to encourage them. They had to rely upon their own devices to develop internally the desire to learn. Many we not successful. Consequently, they were indifferent to education.

I was one of the lucky ones. True to the spirit of a Hoosier, my goal was to be a professional basketball player. I most certainly was indifferent to education. While a junior in high school, my former sixth-grade teacher took me aside and reminded me that there were no professional basketball players five foot three, slow, and lacked the ability to ascend to great heights. He added that I possessed only one attribute that was a saving grace. If I wanted to avoid being poor, I would take advantage of that. I took heed of this mentor. Believe me, being poor, and the fear of being poor, are effective motivators to make the right decisions.

WAY OVER MY HEAD

One very good illustration of this indifference involved a homie who surly had the capabilities for college. In Division 9, at about the age of ten, I came upon him sitting of the bench outside our division, reading a book. He rarely played with us, choosing instead to read. Curiosity, my dearest enemy, caused me to ask what he was reading. He showed me the title. My next dearest enemy, annoyance, caused me to ask what the book was about. It was if I had wakened a sleeping giant. He seemed excited that he could talk about the book. He described aspects of the book that were way over my head. Though I understood little of what he said, I listened intently. I was more fascinated about the excitement he showed. He made good grades in school, but they were most certainly not indicative of his capabilities. He never continued his education after leaving the home, although he did live a good life. He was the perfect example of children with considerable capabilities who were indifferent to education.

WHY?

I recalled another experience that illustrates this indifference. In what I believe was the fourth grade, the teacher used competitive games as strategies to teach the basic subjects. We lined up along the wall, and the teacher asked each a question. Those who incorrectly answered the question had to sit down, while the ones correctly answering continued. Bob and I retired very quickly and continued with our naps. During one of these challenges, the teacher changed the rules slightly. The winner and runner up of the math challenge would get an additional half hour of recess. Wow! We indifferent children woke up and took notice. Bob easily won, and I was runner up. Later, the teacher removed the incentive. We returned to our unmotivated selves. Some years later, during homecoming, I had a talk with one of my former teachers about Bob. He was adopted out of the home by a relative. With his new life and motivators, he made A's in high school and graduated from college. He came back to visit during a homecoming and had a discussion with the teacher about his education at the home. The teacher asked him why he did not make A's while in the home.

Bob answered most appropriately, "There was no reason to."

27

The Secret Society

Of all the peer groups in the home, one stands out as unique, and very strange. At an age of about six years old, several children formed a peer group. Unique about this group was that no other child joined the group after its inception, and to my knowledge, no one wanted to join. It still is a mystery what commonality bonded their alliance. My guess is that they were harboring a secret. If so, that secret will forever remain as such. I called the group The Secret Society.

We lived with this peer group, went to school with them, and participated in sports with them. These were unavoidable contacts. Otherwise, The Secret Society kept pretty much to themselves, rarely if ever joining the rest of us to play. Regardless, I rarely heard of any negative opinions of the members of this peer group. It was if their own little group was their own little world. There was one occasion when they asked me to participate in an activity with them. To better understand this, one should first know about cattle and their affection for pears.

Cattle are harmless but very curious animals. If you enter their pasture, they will take notice and slowly approach. If you run, they will run after you. If you stop running, they will stop. Now, if you are not familiar with this trait, their actions may be misinterpreted as an attempt to do you bodily harm. Their domain, called Forty Acres, was next to the older girls' divisions across the lake. On the other side of Forty Acres was an old pear orchard. It was no longer used, but still produced considerable amounts of very delicious pears. They were so good that the home staff paid good money for them. Harvesting these pears could mean considerable wealth. We were not allowed to visit the pasture and pear orchard. I guess they wanted to prevent us and the cattle to be in near proximity. This pasture was well within sight of the home staff. To access those pears without being seen, one had to go a long way around the cattle's pasture. Optionally, one could take a chance of being seen, by taking a much shorter route directly across the pasture.

Kevin and I took the long route around the pasture and harvested two bushels of pears. Lugging these for the better part of a mile was not very appealing. We decided to take a chance and make our way back thru the cattle's pasture. Upon seeing us, the cattle ran towards us, led by one that was by far the largest. He was obviously the leader. We ran, not knowing their intent, greedily lugging that bushel. The cattle came upon us very quickly and surrounded us. Their leader stood in front of us, blocking our exit. Kevin figured out their real intentions and instructed me to give each a pear. As they munched, we ran with the rest of the pears towards the fence. This seemed to work. However, the cattle made short work of the pears, and again ran after us. Again, the leader blocked our escape. This scenario repeated itself until we reached the fence. Upon reaching the fence, we discovered there were only about half a dozen pears left. Upon leaving that pasture, I could swear the large one was grinning. Now that you know about the cattle, I will get the point of all of this as it pertains to the secret society.

Behind the older boys' divisions is a huge hazelnut tree, its limbs so large that one could easily walk on them like strolling along the sidewalk. I came upon this tree as I was making my way back to the home from the woods. The secret society was playing tree tag. Upon seeing me, they huddled together, occasionally glancing at me. This put me on guard. Obviously, something was being planned. Just as I was leaving, they called me back and asked if I wanted to play tree tag with them. I should have followed my suspicions. However, I was excited about being included into their group. Their leader, a good friend, explained that to play, I first had to demonstrate the capability to jump from tree to tree. My *friend* explained that I had to jump from the hazelnut tree onto an adjoining pine tree, lower myself to the ground, make my way through the bushes to another tree, climb it, and then jump from it onto one of the limbs of that hazelnut tree. I previously had never thought to participate in tree tag, since my anxiety went up the farther the ground I found myself. However, the anticipation of playing with new friends dangerously skewed my decision.

Up the hazelnut tree I went. I jumped onto the top of the pine tree, my weight causing it to bend, gently lowering me among the bushes, a feat we did so often in the woods. Upon landing in the middle of those bushes, I was reminded why playing near that hazelnut tree was avoided. The bushes had thorns, very big thorns! The punishment dealt out by those thorns caused me to scream, and the secret society to laugh. It was obvious my predicament was not by accident. More embarrassed from falling for this prank, than hurt by those thorns, I quickly made my way out of the bushes. This only helped those bushes emphasize why they should be avoided. I yelled out to their leader, asking if he knew about those thorns. He answered in the negative, upon which they all laughed even louder. By this age, we children were not strangers to pranks. When we became the prankees, we always went on with our lives; thinking nothing of it. (LOL) However, this prank begged for revenge as I had to have that painful mercurochrome treatment. I remembered the episode Kevin and I had with the cattle.

One of my partners in playing pranks let it slip to the secret society that the pears in the orchard across the cattle's pasture were worth a fortune to those who could get them. Oops! The secret society took about six bushels with them to the orchard, going the long way around the pasture to avoid being seen by the home staff. They filled the bushels and started back to the home. I had made my way to the orchard, standing next to the fence separating the pasture from the orchard. I thought it was strange that the cattle never approached me as I made my way across their domain. I did notice the large one keeping an eye on me. I yelled out to the secret society that it would be easier to take the pears back to the home the short way, across the pasture. I added that I would keep a watch out for the home staff. I made my way across the pasture. Again, the cattle did not approach me, and again the large one took notice. I pretended to look for the home staff and yelled to the others that the coast was clear. As they were making their way across the pasture, the cattle saw those bushels and stampeded towards them. The secret group panicked and ran. You must give them credit. They kept ahold of those bushels! As with Kevin and I, the large one blocked their path while the other cattle surrounded the group and those pears. Like Kevin, the leader of the secret society figured out what the cattle wanted. He implemented the same strategy Kevin had thought of. It had the same outcome.

I had this sensation we all do when our efforts are rewarded with success. In other words, revenge was mine. Unfortunately, the leader of the secret society was very intelligent. He devised a strategy that could foil my plan. He instructed one in his group to scatter his bushel of pears upon the ground. As the cattle started munching away, the group ran towards the fence with the other bushels. I became very worried. My brilliant plan was about to fail. I then noticed the large one looking at the pears on the ground, then at the pears making their getaway. I had skipped church for the past six years. But I was desperate.

I go down on my knees and prayed, "Please, God, do the right thing."

The large one and I must have been soulmates. He decided several hundred pears to eat were better than the few on the ground and ran towards the group making their escape. The other cattle followed. The secret society experienced the same fate as Kevin and me.

After escaping with just a few pears, the leader of this secret society approached me and asked, "Did you know about those cattle?" My answer was "No." We both laughed.

Those of The Secret Society went their own ways after leaving the home. I am not sure they ever got together like they did while in the home. Perhaps it was the home itself that bonded them during their stay. Regardless, they all are together again; and forever.

28

Sadie

There is a time when we meet to renew acquaintances; to enthusiastically hug all, even those we shared little time; to laugh about those Dear John letters and to laughingly scorn those that were their cause; to recall when your heart was broken and when you broke another's; to recall disappointments and successes; to discuss the should've, could've, would've outcomes; a time to renew that joy of beating your arch enemy, and the sadness of losing to the same; to show sincere interest about the lives of your siblings; a time to bury hatchets, to beg forgiveness for not doing to others what you hoped they would do to you, to forgive all who did not follow those wise words of Jesus; to again laugh about that which we laughed at before, and even that which before we never would never laugh at; to not be embarrassed about exhibiting emotions, and to show sympathy to others when those emotions are bared; to leave a legacy to those you grew up with, to confirm they are indeed your siblings.

Some 40 years after graduating, the theme of our homecoming was the 50s and 60s; the era I grew up in the home. I was approaching the entrance into the dance hall where 50s songs were being played. I recalled another time when I wanted to go to a dance. Instead of attending that homecoming dance, I sought out a lover I depended upon in difficult times while in the home. I found Sadie lying in her special area behind the Greenhouse, undisturbed for all those years. I shared a tear. We were together again. She was as beautiful then as when I first saw her. She did not display her majestic self as she once did in her prime. Her color was now white and gray, and she had grown smaller in stature. She had given so much and now was prepared to meet that fate we all must. We reminisced about a time when our hearts had been broken, and when we listed to those 50s era songs being played at the dance hall. It was time to leave. I got up and walked away without saying a word, glancing back at her with a smile. Sadie returned that sign of love, exactly as she had done when she had comforted me during my times of trouble. We realized we had spent our last time together. We left each other, sharing memories of a day in November when we had depended upon each other for comfort.

It was an era when gentlemen were expected to ask ladies for a date, and the ladies expected to give undeniable hints. You know, when they look at you with that smile all males cannot misinterpret. Then there were the very opposite hints. Enough said! The tradition of boys asking girls was reversed on a day in November. The ladies asked the gentlemen to accompany them for a grand night of dancing. On the day of reckoning, our hearts pounded in expectation of receiving an invitation, and in fear of being rejected. Undeniable hints were being received from one so adored. My expectations of an invitation were very high. Our governess received the invitations. One by one, the names of the fortunate recipients were called out. With a broken heart and a portable transistor radio, I sought out Sadie. Her heart was also broken. Sadie and I snuggled. We cried our troubles away as we listed to the 50s songs of that year.

Not one to easily give up on dreams, the next year found me again copying from one most popular with the ladies, with the intention of attaining popularity. I say 'again' because he was the same sibling I had mimicked while a toddler to gain attention from the adults watching us splash in the wading pool. Following his examples, I took showers more often, got a cool haircut, kept the side burns, combed them often in sight of the ladies, carried a comb in my shirt sleeve, wore tight jeans, greased my hair, and practiced the 'cool' 50s jargons. I realized the ladies were taking notice of my new self, although they seemed to be whispering to each other. I also noticed some of my friends shaking their heads in disbelief. On that day in November, my expectations were again very high. The governess revealed who was invited. I and that transistor radio again sought out Sadie. Sadie was glad to see me again, though sad as to why I sought her company. She had troubles of her own, making it difficult to provide the comfort I had become accustomed to. Again, we snuggled, listening to those 50s songs.

Twice tried, twice failed. I thought about giving up trying to get an invitation. However, one of my siblings seemed to believe he was an expert in the ways of the ladies. He suggested I had only to compliment ladies on their attributes, even if they were little white lies. With confidence in his expertise, I forged ahead. I congratulated one on her dress, insensitive to the fact that it was revealing. She certainly interpreted that compliment somewhat differently than intended. Another was the benefactor of a compliment on her hairstyle. In fact, it looked like a squirrel had crawled up and died on her head. She must have known that. I do not believe she ever talked to me for rest of the year. To one I secretly believed was my true love, I took that leap of faith for boys our age. I told her she was beautiful. Actually, it was the only compliment which was truly true.

She gave me that look interpreted as "You never noticed me before. Just what do you want?"

Undeterred, I continued: a compliment for all. On that day in November, the invitations were again sent out. With so many compliments, to so many, surely this would be the year. Again, Sadie and I snuggled together. My old companion's health had deteriorated considerably, but she still wanted to console me. For different reasons, we were filled with regrets, trying to forget. Together, we listened to those 50s songs. I expressed regret to Sadie on her troubles and thanked her for the comfort she gave this unfortunate soul.

Times of desperation create strategies of a sultry nature. It was my senior year and my last chance to realize my dream. In previous occasions, I had sought the advice of those who I believed more expert than I on these matters. Now I was desperate. I decided to take the bull by the horns. Unfortunately, I had no idea how to do this. The how was discovered as I was taking a shortcut through the stage in the back of the school's gym. I came upon the most popular boy in the school, in an intimate embrace, to put it lightly, with one who was not his girlfriend. We never tell on our friends! Fortuitously, the girl and I were mortal enemies. I cornered this girl and threatened to disclose what I had seen, unless she did what I wanted. She gave me a look of complete disgust, which in hindsight is understandable. She agreed, which in hindsight is an opportunity lost. I told her she had to invite me to the Sadie Hawkins dance.

Her look changed from one of disgust to "What?".

My last chance arrived with the greatest of expectations and extreme confidence In what must be the commitments of commitments, I forced myself to be a good boy; avoiding demerits. With my savings, I purchased a new pair of Levies. I took a bubble bath followed with some cologne, greased and combed my hair back. My friends looked at me as if I had finally lost it completely. This was probably not far from the truth. Upon receiving the invitations, the governess called out my name. I quickly opened the invitation. The message in the invitation was an offer for me to kiss a specific part of this girl's physique. For what we believed would be one last time, Sadie and I spent time together. She had lived a long and giving life and now was willing to comfort me one last time. I realized that she was the only one who had invited me to that grand dance. We spent the night listening to the 50s songs. Finally, the batteries gave out, and the music came no more. So was my chance to attain my dream. I said goodbye to Sadie.

29

Home Staff Are Human

DO NOT WALK ON THE GRASS!

Our perceptions of others change as we grow older, fatter and wiser. Life experiences cause completely different takes of people than we had long ago. While at the home, my perception of the home staff was they were far from human. Maybe teenagers can identify with that. That perception changed in my junior year at the home, helped by one of my dearest friends.

Barry had and has a remarkable talent for writing. This proved extremely useful for him, and us, to pass those ugly, college English classes. It also proved extremely useful on Halloween. I was punished for walking on the grass. I said that right! This witch of a governess punished me walking on the grass! I say that lovingly of course. The punishment was to miss the Halloween hayride. It was an activity she knew that I thoroughly enjoyed. Witch! One of the home staff in charge of this hayride, one I would later call Good, recognized the absurdly of this punishment. He stepped in and gave me an out. If I could satisfactorily explain in a narrative why I should not walk on the grass, he would allow me to go on the hay ride.

Realizing my limitations for writing, I was resigned to accept my fate. Barry came to the rescue. He offered to help write the narrative. After about twenty minutes writing, we had two reasons why we should not walk on the grass. One was we were ordered not to. The other was we were ordered not to. Again, I decided to accept my fate. Barry convinced me to forge ahead. We were very creative on reasons why we should not walk on the grass. Most were so ridiculous that I decided to just take my medicine and miss the hayride. Again, Barry came to the rescue, convincing me that I could not lose anything by submitting the narrative. I submitted the narrative.

The time of the hayride was near. We had not heard back from the person in charge of the hayride. I decided to take the bull by the horns and approach the home staff for a decision. I marched over to the administration building. Everyone had left for the day; subsequently it was futile trying to find the one in charge. As I was leaving disappointed, I heard loud laughter from one of the offices. I softly opened the door and glanced in. Several of the staff were gathered around a person reading something from a piece of paper. After they stopped laughing and continued reading, I realized it was our narrative explaining why we should not walk on the grass. I knocked on the door to get their attention. They all turned around with that surprised look common among us children when caught with our hands in the cookie jar. I asked if I could go on the hayride. They quickly indicated I could, trying to show seriousness in that answer. I closed the door but stopped momentarily and listened. They continued reading the narrative and again laughed, even louder than before. I realized these home staff were only human, with the same humor we children possessed. They just could not express this in front of the children. Unfortunately, a miscommunication between the enforcer and our governess resulted in no hayride. It was worth it though. I discovered the home staff were human.

GOOD AND EVIL
One moment tested my realization home staff were human. Good and Evil are worthy adversaries, battling throughout history to win souls of

people. One basks in its successes and our failures. The other exult in its successes and ours. I was witness to such a combat. One summer was filled with idleness and boredom. Such was the ideal opportunity for Evil. Good joined the combat. Good was invited into the heart of a newly hired staffer. We will call the bored child Evil. The newly hired staffer we will call Good. Evil discovered that experienced home staff had all left for summer vacations. This left oversight to the inexperienced overseer, Good. Those of you who had substitute teachers know the opportunity that presented itself.

Evil decided to turn a quiet, boring evening into one of excitement. Old 45 records were sold to an avid collector. An electric razor was sold to one who actually needed it. It was near July 4 and firecrackers were readily available. Two huge boomers were purchased from a small town near the home. A lighter was then obtained from the locker of a friend that smoked. These were hidden in a fire escape attached to the Town Hall, adjacent to the rooms where children gathered in the evening to dance to that old juke box.

Evil measured the time to run from the fire escape to the side door of the Town Hall gym: about three seconds. The burning time of the boomers' wicks was determined, about an inch per second. The wicks on the two boomers were cut to six and three seconds respectively. These boomers and the lighter were hidden in the fire escape attached to Town Hall.

Evil waited for a time when the children were at Town Hall. He advised the governess that he was going to take a bath. The bathtub was filled with hot water, and the volume of an old transistor radio turned up. Evil then exited out the back door. Evil retrieved the boomers and the lighter from the fire escape at Town Hall. The six-second boomer was lit and thrown in the fire escape. Evil laughed, as he knew the sound of the explosion bouncing off the metal walls would ensure considerable amplification, and scare the hell out of anyone nearby. Evil ran to the side door of the Town Hall gym, being careful to count off exactly three seconds. The three-second boomer was then lit and thrown inside the gym. The gym was small, and the sound of the explosion bouncing off its walls would also ensure considerable amplification. Evil then ran, with a capital R, back to Division 29, where the bath, and the alibi, were waiting. On the way, Evil laughed when the boomers went off, signaling the triumph of Evil over Good. Evil entered the division, through the back door, up to the bathroom, quickly discarded his clothes, tossed the lighter behind a steam register, and jumped into the bathtub.

An instant after jumping in the bathtub, the bathroom door swung open. There was Good! It was without a doubt the most astonishing moment of Evil's existence at the home.

Evil held out his arms in a gesture best interpreted as, "How could you possibly know who did it, and how could you possibly have made it to the division within a split second of me?"

Good laughed at that gesture. He told Evil, "You will have to do much better than that while I am on guard. Now there is no rule about setting off firecrackers, but there is a rule about having a lighter. Where is it?"

"Behind the heat register. How did you know I used a lighter?"

"I didn't, until you just told me."

Good retrieved the lighter and started to leave.

Evil asked, "Am I going to be punished?"

"You have been punished."

Evil thought about what Good had said for a while. All that can be reckoned is the punishment was the realization Good had triumphed over Evil. To this day, I cannot fathom how Good could have known it was me, and it is even more perplexing just how he made it to the division within a split second after I did. One thing is for sure, Evil never again tried anything while Good was on guard, even when there were ample opportunities.

THE JITTER BUG

The best lesson, as regards the human side of home staff, was taught by an ancient lady that oversaw the kitchen crew. Several of we boys were members of the crew, charged with the tedious task of cleaning the dining room and washing dishes. Our ancient overseer barked out orders like a staff Sargent, slapping the table with a spatula each time to get our attention. My take on her was she had everything to do with business, and nothing to do with being human. I cannot speak for the others, but I quickly followed those orders. I feared she may keel over if she ever got upset. One of those orders was to retrieve a bag of cherries. It was not an unexpected chore, but had an unexpected outcome.

The cherries were put in what appeared to be an old wooden bucket. She had me mash those cherries, pits and all, with a potato smasher. Sugar, water, and some substances she brought from home were added. This mixture was locked away in one of the cabinets. Now I am a hillbilly, from a family of moonshiners. I knew well what eventually would come out of that cabinet. About every two weeks we retrieved the bucket, stirred the contents, and placed it back in the cabinet. Each time we did this, I had a good laugh, knowing what eventually would result. The kitchen job was probably the least liked of all jobs at the Home. We seniors desperately looked forward to the last day we had to do those dishes. That day finally came. We were excited, ready to leave for our division to celebrate. Our staff Sargent ordered we seniors to stay over. She retrieved the bucket and filtered the contents thru some cheese cloth. We all enjoyed a glass of about the best cherry wine I have ever tasted; and I have tasted a few. Surprised and astonished would be an understatement of how we felt to have an opportunity to drink wine. Our benefactor had on the outside a charade of being a stern, inhuman person. Inside she was just a wonderful, elderly lady. She proved to be more wonderful than elderly.

The most endearing quality of that wine caused effects we teenagers were not supposed to experience. It was, most definitely, full bodied; a description related to its alcohol content. Our Staff Sargent realized this and allowed us to drink only half a glass. She ignored our pleas to have more. We thanked her, and left for Division 27. We laughed as we made our way to our division. I noticed the others laughing louder than I. When we arrived at the division, our governess asked me why I was still wearing an apron. I went back to the kitchen to return it.

Very loud music was heard upon entering the kitchen. It was from the radio we listened to while working. I glanced into the dining room.

Our wonderful Staff Sargent had moved some of the chairs and tables, turning the room into a small dance hall. She was dancing by herself to the music of rock and roll! I was so taken back by this spectacle that I just stood there in awe. She noticed me. I told her I was just returning the apron. She laughed and asked me not to tell anyone about the dance hall. I told her I would not. She then said I could pour myself another glass of wine, surely as a bribe. I did, and she did. As if I were a bartender, she revealed some interesting experiences of her life, which confirmed her human side. We sipped the wine during these revelations. She told me of a time when the ladies danced with the service men, before they faced only what those most brave could. She mentioned several dances. Some I sort of recognized from the big band music. I told her I never learned how to dance. She jumped up, took my hand, and onto the dance floor we went. To the music of an all-time favorite of mine, *Ain't That a Shame*, she taught me the two-step. To the best of my recollection it was just that, repeated over and over, but in different directions. She tried to teach me the cha, cha. Rock and roll music was ill-suited for that. We could not find any music that was to the familiar *one two three, one two tree*; the waltz. She started to hum a waltz. I recognized it as a very famous waltz, from my experiences in the dance band. Encouraged by the effects of that wine, I joined in humming. Together we hummed while she waltzed, and I 'waltzed'. By this time, I was convinced that I had missed my calling. I loved those dances! In getting in the spirit of the moment, I mentioned that my mother had taught me this dance: The Charleston. Without any music we did The Charleston, or at least an interpretation of it. That dance I enjoyed the most. She continued to dance, and I continued to 'dance', for a long time, aided by refreshments of cherry wine. Finally, the song that helped spawn rock and roll came on the radio: Rock Around the Clock. She jumped up, dragged me onto the dance floor once more. She tried to teach me a dance with a very strange name: The Jitter Bug. The sight of a ninety plus elderly lady doing that dance stayed with me for a long time. To that tune she tried to teach me this weird move where she rolled over my back. Aided by that cherry wine, we ended up on the floor. As we sat there laughing, we noticed the enforcer nearby. He was also laughing. He told me I had been reported as missing, and I should return to the division. As I left, I heard him tell this wonderful, young lady that he would drive her home. She giggled like a school girl!

The alcohol in that wine made its effects known. Attempting to manage the three steps leading from the kitchen resulted in me face down on the ground. As my face was entrenched in the dirt, my mind was wondering why my legs were not taking steps. As I lay there, I noticed some chairs in the trash bin next to the kitchen. The effects of that wine must have awakened my sensitive side. I felt sorry for those chairs. After all, they had supported us so much in our time of need. It was so unfair to simply discard them when they grew old. I decided to save them. I could rescue only three. I still have this vision of three chairs making their way across the home grounds. The journey back to my division was somewhat affected by that wine. It was two steps forward, one to the side, a couple backwards, and others not in a straight line. I believe those steps were weird renditions of those dance steps; more accurately, the two-step. In between the dining hall and my division was the fountain where our small gang had confirmed our commitment to a pledge by eating a bug. At least one of us did. The fountain was not in the way of a normal journey to my division. It was directly in the zig zag path I was taking. The strange journey caused me and the chairs to end up in the pool of water beneath that fountain. I do not remember much after that. Two of my siblings told me they found me walking around the pool in the water, talking to the statue. They interrupted my discussion with the statue and dragged me to the division, and upstairs to my bed. Two married couples oversaw we senior boys. I recalled them standing over me. As I was wondering why the room was spinning, I heard the man say, "I think he is drunk"! The woman said something to the effect, "They don't pay me enough for this job"!

FRIDAY NIGHTS

Sooner or later we all learned that our overseers were human. This was ever so evident of our governess in Division 14. She had a son, a flying

Marine. We learned to sing that Air Force Song starting with "Off we go, into the wild blue yonder." When her son visited, we all sang that song. What made her a favorite to many of us was her philosophy about children. She believed children should spend their time being children. She had us do some minor chores in the morning. After that she kicked us out of the division, much to our liking. She then spent the rest of the day cleaning the Division, doing chores we were supposed to do. She played the Marine Air Force song on the Victrola while she cleaned the Division. Two experiences are illustrative of her human qualities.

Our wonderful governess had an obsession to protect us, at all costs. This was ever so evident to a newly hired home staffer. A couple of us caught his attention; for what I cannot recall. He chased we offenders across the home grounds. We thought we were safe upon reaching our division. He followed us. He grabbed us, and proceeded to drag us from the division, probably to the enforcer's office. Our protector came out of her room. She noticed this man dragging us. She screamed. Her words were something to the effect that no one, that is no one, comes into her Division without her permission, and no one touches her kids. She then ordered this man to leave. The man not only was extremely large, he outranked her. He continued to drag us and told her that he would come into the Division whenever he wanted. Wrong response! Our guardian angel picked up a broom and proceeded to beat this poor unsuspecting man. He tried to cover up, but there is nothing more fearsome than this protector with a broom and a temper. He was forced to hastily make his way to the door, covering up his head. He broke the outside door in a hasty retreat. Once outside he apologized to our protector. We laughed, and I believed this man laughed. We stopped laughing when she turned her anger to us for doing whatever we did. For the life of me, I cannot recall what that was to make this man angry. It cost us two days on the punishment chair. We admired her for her interest in protecting us, at all cost.

The most unforgettable human aspect of this governess was revealed each Friday. It was her night and she made sure it was perfect. She scheduled us to take a shower, making sure we kept right on schedule. She organized the chairs around our black and white TV, then assigned seats. All of us received a bag of popcorn, followed with the all too familiar warning "I do not want to hear a peep for the next hour." Trust me, there was no peep. It was Friday night wrestling! I have been in bars during sports events. The yelling and emotions exhibited there were nothing compared to what our governess showed. Friday night was her night!

What happened one night caused her to exhibit that unique human characteristic. It was an era of live TV, meaning everyone saw everything that happened as it happened; even that which was not intended to be seen. Her favorite wrestler jumped from the ropes of the ring to body slam another. He slipped, and fell on his back. He did not move. The other wrestler started to pin him. After recognizing the condition of his adversary, he quickly left the ring. The injured wrestler lay there for a long time. Finally, the TV switched to a movie. We asked our governess what happened. She cried and ordered us to bed. We later found out her favorite wrestler had been severely injured. Some aspects of live TV were not that entertaining.

30

Sex Education

I will not say sex was on the mind of us boys most of the time, but my hormones can. It was an era when nudity was a crime, and partially nudity was forbidden. Subsequently, there was little opportunity to really see the girls, if you know what I mean. There were some interesting occasions we tried; times dictated by our hormones.

WHAT AN OPPORTUNITY!
The basement rooms of Morton Memorial High School had windows, making it easy to view any inside. Some of these rooms served as locker rooms for the boys and girls. These were on opposite sides of the high school of course. The windows for the girl's locker rooms were easily recognized. They were painted to discourage peeking. They were painted on the inside I might add. We boys were perfect gentlemen. Peeking was not on our minds. (LOL) Such an opportunity came about because of the home staff's belief that life as a janitor fit my capabilities.

Children were assigned to trade shops that the home staff believed would be good matches to their capabilities. For example, the smarter children were placed in the print shop, those who took their appearance seriously were placed in the barber shop, those who showed an interest in farming were placed at the farm. At the expense of insulting honorable trades, all others were placed in the green house or in the school as janitors. My indifference to education must have been obvious to the home staff. I spent my entire home life in the latter two trades.

In my sophomore year, while working as a janitor, a real janitor woke me from my usual nap. I was told to remove all the items from the sports equipment rooms. They were going to paint the shelves. While removing items on the top shelf in the girls' equipment room, I noticed the wall separating their equipment and locker rooms did not extend all the way to the ceiling. Normal children may not make anything of that. I did. I made my way over the top shelf and to the top of that wall. I found myself with a bird's eye view of the girls' locker room! My imagination soared to new heights realizing this was where they undressed, took showers, and then dressed! As a good Christian boy, I never thought twice about what that little guy on my shoulder was saying. (LOL). I came back to earth when I realized it would be impossible to take advantage of the obvious opportunity.

I mentioned this discovery to Charles, a friend who was an excellent schemer. He thought for a long time.

"Do you think we could — "?, you know what.

"Impossible."

"No offense, but you seem to give up to easily. Can you get the keys to their equipment room."

"Sure. I am a janitor. They keep all the keys hanging on a wall in their office. They never notice any missing."

"Good. Tomorrow there is a track meet. Everyone will be at the track. Get the keys and meet me by the gym next to the girls dressing rooms."

There we were, inside the equipment room, surveying the possibilities. We joked as we made plans to take advantage of that unfinished wall. We settled on this plan. We would hide under the bottom shelf until the girls were in the showers, then make our way to the top shelf; hopefully see what we dreamed about, or saw in some eight-page bibles.

Charles insisted on a dry run, which reveals his ability as a schemer. Later that week, the keys to the locker rooms were appropriated, and we found ourselves in the girl's equipment room.

We had just gone inside the equipment room when we heard the outside hallway door open. We dove under the bottom shelf, our scare gauge topping out. In walked the music teacher, a person more wonderful than can be described. She opened a case holding what I believe was a flute or oboe. She started playing! Why she chose the equipment room to play is still puzzling. We kept very quiet. After about half an hour, Charles started giggling about our predicament. As so often we children did, when one laughed, the other would join in, oftentimes without realizing why. We laughed very quietly, and not at all when the music teacher quit playing. Several times she looked around as if she heard something. Finally, she left. After she left we laughed out loud for a while. We continued our dry run.

As we were leaving I remarked, "That was too close. She could have caught us. I am not sure about doing this."

"Well, I think we can do it."

Being a coward, I responded, "I don't know."

"Well, I want to try. Can you get the keys Friday?"

"Sure. Why Friday?"

"The girls usually play softball right after school on Friday."

This was one of the few instances when the home supported a girl's sport. I appropriated the keys for Charles, and watched as he made his way into the girl's locker room. I went outside and anxiously waited to find out what happened. He came out of the school with a strange look.

I asked him, several times, "What happened? Did you see anything?"

He refused to reveal what happened. After the umpteenth time of harassment, he related this to me, "I hid under the bottom shelf. The girls came into the room, got the bats, gloves, and softballs, then left. They did not even notice me. After the game, they put the equipment back and went into the dressing room. I heard Miss Williams (the gym teacher) tell the girls they could take a shower, or go directly to their divisions. She told them she had to be elsewhere, locked the equipment room, and left."

We knew where she "had to be." A rumor was she and one of the teachers were hot on each other. We decided to investigate, as they both seemed to stay after school a lot, at the back of the stage next to the gym no doubt. We peeked. They were doing what we boys and girls did, only much better, and around more bases than we ever got.

Charles continued, "I waited until I could hear some of the girls in the locker room. I climbed up on the shelf and looked."

By this time, I was excited beyond excited, "Really! What did you see. Tell me what you saw!"

"I saw a girl take off her bra!"

I realized Charles saw what most of us only dreamed about.

"Oh man, I missed it. I should have been there."

I noticed Charles was not sharing my excitement. I knew him well, and could tell when he was bothered.

I inquired, "What is wrong?"

He said nothing for a long time. Being my annoying self, I kept with the question. After the umpteenth time, he blurted out, "It was Jane, my sister!"

I laughed. He did not. After listening to me laugh for about half an hour, he joined in laughing. We spent the rest of the evening laughing at that misfortune. I wanted to do what Charles had done. I chickened out, and I am sticking with that story.

THE TUNNELS

The home took great pains to separate the girls and boys. They also took great pains to make sure there was sufficient oversight when the boys and girls comingled. Couples could sit together during a show presented in Lincoln Hall. Even then they were scrutinized closely by the home staff. I might add, we younger children also scrutinized them; at least during the news cast. All parents have the urge to make sure their children are acting appropriately. For the home, this appeared to be an obsession. However, love cannot be denied. The children devised strategies that would allow them some quality time together outside the prevue of the staff. Tragically, two very lovable couples crossed the line. When it became obvious they had, the home overreacted. As unbelievable as it may seem, the home ceased all activities that allowed even the shortest times for opposite sexes to share time alone. More unbelievable, this included holding hands during school time. Popular dating spots were the stairways at Morton Memorial High School, during the short five minutes between classes. Thanks to the wisdom of our teachers, no one was 'caught'. The old Civil War Theatre became a popular dating spot. It had many hiding places. That seemed inappropriate. It also served as the church.

I doubt other children knew about the dating places I enjoyed. One spot was discovered when I enjoyed the enchantment of the home at night while a toddler. Water flowed from Lake Graham down a waterfall, through a stone-lined tunnel, exiting onto a stone ledge, then falling into a brook. That stone ledge was well hidden by pine trees. Although close to a walkway, it was impossible to see beyond those pine trees. The water trickling down into a brook provided soft music for love making. When I worked at the home, I told the enforcer about this place. The next day found myself and others doing some heavy trimming of those pine trees. Another place was where I kissed my prom date. If you climb up the side of the valley where the brook flowed, there is a sidewalk, well hidden from the surrounding grounds. It is a mystery why that walk was even there, as it led to nowhere, except to a very magical sweetheart tree. Underneath that tree we had our first and only kiss.

The strict rules about interacting with the opposite sex brought about desperation, with a capital D. This desperation brought out the wonderful initiatives and imaginations of the girls. The home had very large and well-constructed utility tunnels. They were compliments of a popular 1930's job program. The tunnels started from the power plant, and spanned out, connecting the plant with all the buildings. Judging from their quality, the people working in the 1930's job program took great pride in their work. One could easily walk upright through them! The girls reminded we boys that while these tunnels were used to connect the power plant to the divisions, they inadvertently connected the divisions with each other. The boys could end up in their divisions through that network of tunnels. Crime needs motive and access, which was ever too obvious in this case. The boys mapped those tunnels, using a color code. This was necessary to make sure they ended up in the basement of the appropriate girl's division. The entrances to the tunnels were always locked; from the basement side of the tunnels. Not a problem for our girls. During the years of dating in the tunnels, no one ended up like our two lovers responsible for the home's drastic measures to prevent teen pregnancy.

With a place to date outside the eyes of home staff, one could see a dramatic change in the demeanor of the children. They were much happier, and seemed to be able to focus on things other than necking. I may be kidding about that! My prom date must have had a concern about teen pregnancy. Remember that creed: we never told, never! Carrie had the far sightedness to know the dangers of teen pregnancy, and broke that creed. She surely sacrificed her popularity among we children to further a cause much more important. Kudos to her. The next day two of the home staff watched the tunnel entrance and exit. They took down names. It was the end of dating in the tunnels. Fortunately, I had taken the day off. Carrie pleaded me to come clean. To this day I cannot understand the rationale of doing that.

STUFF DREAMS ARE MADE OF

Since we are talking about Carrie, she was instrumental to the success of my last creative attempt to make an otherwise boring moment memorable. It was the weekend of the year when the girls showcased their design talents. Our girls were extremely talented. It was a huge event. The event took place in the high school gym, located in the center of the school. We boys fantasized that the girls modeled unmentionables and joked about peeking. The janitors were wise to our intentions. They made extreme efforts to prevent inappropriate viewing. I know because I worked as a janitor and helped them. The gym was in the center of the school, surrounded by hallways. It was easy to block viewing simply by blocking entrances to the hallways surrounding the gym. The only possible way to view this event was through the windows above the gym, on the school roof. The janitors had this covered, literally. The upper gym windows were covered with a large black mat. Just to make sure, the windows to the roof were all locked.

A rumor was making its rounds that a very pretty girl, you know who, would be modeling bras. Now, if you had to pick a girl to model bras, she would be the choice of every male at the home. This sparked the interest of many. Very few times are there opportunities custom made for success. First, we had the sexiest girl in the school modeling bras. Second, we had boys with hormones making their decisions. Finally, one of us had a job which allowed access to the keys of the windows. It would have been an insult to all good old American boys if what follows was not undertaken.

The keys to a window leading to and off the roof were obtained. A friend of mine stood in the hallway. He informed whoever passed by that for fifteen cents, they would be able to see what we believed was Carrie half naked. Those that took the bait, and I do not recall any that refused it, were led to the top floor, over to the window leading to the roof. The window was unlocked and opened. With an enthusiasm rarely observed, the victims made their way across the roof to those gym windows, lifted the covers, and peeked down. After all were on the roof, the windows were closed and locked. We then ran down to the hall outside the gym and yelled through the door that some boys were on the roof peeking. Not able to see the girls modeling or the boys on the roof, I do not know what happened. To this day, I cannot fathom how those boys got down from that roof. There was some evidence how they did. There were very narrow walls leading up to the roof from the bathrooms on the top floor. The windows in two of those bathrooms were broken. I also know there was a large oak tree near the school, with limbs that extended near the roof. I had used that route several times. For unknown reasons, these boys did not chase us for that prank. Perhaps they recognized genius, or knew we would soon be history. It was near graduation.

THE CRIME OF THE CENTURY

During my early years, the home staff must have believed I would make it as a chef. Boy, were they wrong! During my tenure of helping the cooks, I witnessed what may be the crime of the century. It reminds me of a popular story involving a magical kingdom. The inhabitants of the kingdom enjoyed happiness beyond description. Until a white Knight on a white horse came visiting. His arrival sparked events that destroyed that happiness.

The home was that happy kingdom for a time. The boys and girls could comingle. There was a date night, and dancing at Town Hall. We held hands openly and innocently necked at activities. It was truly a magical time. The Knight appeared, disguised as the crew helping the cooks.

One of the chores for children in the kitchen was to participate in a somewhat strange ritual. Enough food had to prepared for hundreds of children. Consequently, extremely large steam vats were used to cook the food. The kitchen crew stirred the food in those large vats. When it was time to do this, the one responsible for this task accompanied a cook to the pantry. Some substance was retrieved from a box whose label was hidden using tape. The cook filled a large glass with a substance from that box. As she did this, she laughed and said "for the boys". She then filled another glass with another substance, laughing while she said, "for the girls". She then had us stirring the food add those substances. Inquiries about those ingredients were always met with a response "Never mind."

As we were also the beneficiaries of what we were mixing, our kindness enemy told us to taste what was being mixed into the main course. It had the God-awfulness taste. To spare us and our homies from that taste, we pretended to mix it into the main course. The potato bins were the recipients of those ingredients.

About two years later, the hormones of two lovers ran amuck. They confirmed their feelings for one another in a way that crossed the line, at least during the 50s. To prevent further occurrences, the home overreacted. They eliminated date night, prevented us from dancing, or even holding hands. The happiness of our magical kingdom was destroyed. I never thought much about a connection between our act of omitting the strange substances from the meals, those lovers, and the happiness of our kingdom. I discovered this connection several years after graduating from the home. I was teaching at a school close to Knightstown, and lived in Knightstown. It was also the town where the home cooks lived. One shared memories about the home and those substances.

She revealed that the substances added to the main course were to reduce the hormones in the boys, and slow the development in the girls. What? It occurred to me that by eliminating those substances, the boy's hormones must have gone unchecked, and the girls must have developed much faster. Perhaps this hastened the efforts of the two lovers, the over reaction by the home, and finally the destruction of the happiness of our kingdom. Judging from the behaviors of the boys before and after this crime, that substance was wholly ineffective. For the girls, I noticed their cup size increased. I may be joking about that! I wonder if parents give their children these substances? I would like to apologize to all for eliminating these substances.

31

Pets

ome life was typical of an institution steeped in rules and a rigid structure. The children could be like kids, only as far as the practical rules applied. For example; one ivory tower rule disallowed climbing trees. However; the governesses were very good at looking the other way. The practical rule was we could be kids, as long as we were out of sight and mind of the governesses. Another ivory tower rule was that not pets were allowed. There were two instances of the practical rule that I remember very well.

FREEDOM
Two of the senior boys captured two very large birds. Details of this memory excluded the exact species. I believe they were hawks. When the senior boys took the birds out to the pasture, we small children assembled to watch. The hawks were trained to fly off, then return at the sound of a whistle. While this may have been characterized as 'cool' to many, I found this to be very odd. The hawks could easily fly off to freedom when they were released. Instead, they chose to return to captivity. They

were enticed to do this by rewarding their return with the promise of a treat. As I watched this spectacle; I could not help but to compare these hawks to our life in the home. These hawks were trained by whistles. We children were also trained by whistles. The hawks refused freedom, choosing captivity instead; for no more than to be fed. We children were captivated by the love the home provided. Though we all cherished freedom, more so than children outside the home, we never 'flew away.'

One day we were watching the senior boys with the hawks. It was the end of the school year. It was also the end of the time these senior boys would be at the home. They followed the same sequence of events as before. However; when they released the hawks, the senior boys never blew the whistle. We watched as these hawks circled for a while, then realized their freedom in the woods next to the pasture. We young children cheered. I could not help to believe that there would be a time we could 'fly away.'

OUR ONLY PETS

We boys had pet baby turtles, taken from the muddy end of Lake Graham. They were easy pickings. We waited until their large, scary, snapping mothers were busy, then whisked away the pick of the litter. We cared for these small snappers like all pet owners did for their darlings. Their favorite food was the pesky flies that habituated our division. We removed a wing, then let the fly loose near our pets. With about twenty to thirty children, and each with about two turtles, this feeding strategy was quite effective in ridding the division of those pesky flies. We entered each in the turtle Olympics. Circles of various sizes were drawn on the brick-laid road wounding itself behind our Divisions. Each size was scaled to resemble the Olympic races, such as the 100-yard dash, the 200-yard dash, and my personal favorite, kill yourself just trying to finish mile. Our miniature athletes were placed in the center. On that well-known "ready, get set, go" signal, we set them loose. Normally they would simply sit still. We enticed our miniature heroes to dash outside the circles using flies caught in our Division. The first outside the circle was the winner. A benefit of this was we rid the Divisions of those pesky flies.

However, I digress. The real story is about a dog which became the only real pet many of us had.

QUEENIE

I was spending a week at camp. I confiscated a couple of hot dogs from the kitchen and made my way to a sandy path alongside the small stream that wound itself around the camp. A small fire was used to roast the hot dogs. The wild outdoors created a most appealing atmosphere to enjoy them. As I was about to enjoy the fruits of my efforts, I heard growling. I glanced over and noticed a dog. Later there would be no doubt it was a female dog. She lay on her belly, obviously eyeing those hot dogs. Her appearance revealed that she had spent very little, if any, time with humans. Her fur was thick, long and scraggly, with lumps of whatever. It was obvious the cold winters altered her comfort very little. Her long claws and teeth were proof why her kind survived all these eons. She was extremely quick; something I later found out when I held out a hot dog to her from my hand. My hand was very close to being food. Any prey would be in great danger if they dared to come to close the this little darling. The slightest sound triggered her defense mechanism, and that which recognizes an opportunity for food. She was also at the top of the echelon of her kind. Other wild dogs in the area took off when she voiced her displeasure at them entering her domain. She never accepted my offering. I left one hot dog on a log and left. That night, while sitting by a camp fire near the stream, I thought about her. She probably was a lot like we homies. She was probably a victim of abuse, abandonment, poverty, and circumstance. However, there were significant differences. I contemplated those differences.

Our daily worries were not whether shelter and care would be provided. These were most worrisome for our beast of the wild. We were victims of charity. All that she had were gained thru her own efforts. At first, I had a great deal of sympathy for her. After some thought however, I realized that she was indeed the fortunate one. Of all we children cherished, freedom was at the top of the list. In return for the care we were provided, we sacrificed freedom. Surely this is true for all children. She was quite the opposite. She had her freedom. In return, she sacrificed the opportunity to have shelter and care provided to her. I envied her.

Think about this. To keep her freedom, and her life, she learned to care for herself. That lesson was one most of we children wished we had learned before leaving the Home. Never again would she be threatened by that which our homeless, and probably some of we children, suffer. Is that not what all of us would like to have? In fact, I doubt many of us would gain that in our lifetime.

Eventually, we children were sent out into a world that we had never lived. For many, it would take time to adapt. For some, this was not easy. For a few, it was impossible. She always lived in that world she would spend a lifetime. She never had to deal with adapting. She indeed was the fortunate one. I wished I could have followed in her steps. Back to the story.

Each day I stole, oops, I mean borrowed, hot dogs from our camp kitchen. I went down near the stream and waited for her to appear. She always did. I believe her den must have been in that area. She always refused to approach me for those hot dogs. When I went back to camp, I left behind one of those hot dogs. This continued for several days. Each day she would come closer as I entered her domain. Initially she snarled and displayed that which protected her kind. Eventually she would not snarl or show those teeth. It was clear she was starting to trust me. On the last day of camp, she came close enough to grab the hot dogs from my hands. I held one out. That phrase "in the blink of an eye." would not do justice to her quickness. She grabbed the hot dogs along with part of my fingers, and ran off. I thought it would be the last time I would see her. Later that summer, I had another opportunity to attend camp; this time for two weeks. I got some hot dogs and went to the same spot near the stream. I never held on to the expectation she would be there. After an hour or two, she appeared. She was now wagging her tail slowly, that universal sign of friendship. She casually walked up to me, gently took the hot dog, and walked away. One day I held out my other hand over her head as she was taking the hot dog. She protested at first, but after several times of gently touching her head she allowed it. This went on the rest of the week. During the last day at camp, I freely petted her while she licked my hand. She grabbed the hot dogs and off she went. I was sure it would be the last time I would see her.

The next summer I decided to take a chance that she would still be there. To my amazement, she appeared. She fearlessly wagged her tail. I hugged her as she licked my face. Eventually, she became the pet of the camp ground. We cut her hair and shortened her claws. We left her teeth alone. You know why. Later that summer, she provided us with four small surprises. We children enjoyed our only real pets for the remainder of the summer. We named her Quennie.

32

Sports

That Morton excelled in sports during the early 50s would be an understatement. Our school was extremely small, at least one third of the schools against which we competed. Yet we held our own in all sports. Additionally, most of the schools were rural, educating children of farmers. Some of those children were removed from school in the spring and fall for planting and harvesting. Consequently, they missed a lot of school, and took longer to graduate. It was not uncommon for us to play against grown men. Regardless, we did very well. Our efforts were very memorable. During my senior year, the state made a rule that children older than nineteen could not participate in sports without approval. In sort of a last hurrah, we won the league title in basketball, the only time during Morton's history that was accomplished. There were many wonderful memories of successes in sports. I must admit however that my fondest memories were also the funniest memories, from our not so successful efforts.

OUR FIRST BASEBALL GAME

Enrollment in the home had been declining. Fielding a complete football team became impossible. The home decided to switch to baseball. This sudden switch created some interesting memories.

It was an era when our imaginations created much more interesting times than possibly could be experienced from watching TV. While children outside the home probably went to baseball games, or watched it on TV, we never did. Our total knowledge of the game was that gained from playing sand lot ball. The rules between the sand lot ball we played, and organized baseball, proved to be slightly different; to put it mildly. The transition from football to baseball was anything but smooth.

The first problem was our attire. We had none. Our football shoes became our baseball shoes. It took only about two trips around the bases in those clodhoppers to appreciate the difference between them and baseball shoes. With no way to get baseball shoes, we put our tennis shoes to good use. Our track coach had been at the home for many, many years. He knew of some old 1937 uniforms and gloves that had long been archived. He got those out, dusted them off, and there we were, looking like a team from 1937.

The uniforms were made of heavy, scratchy wool, which during the summer did not make them popular. They were so baggy we resembled a bunch of homeless children, as ironic as that may seem. We never cared about how we looked; we were ecstatic just to get uniforms. The first baseman and catcher were provided new gloves. The rest of us had to use old baseball gloves that had been dragged from archive with those 1937 uniforms. The difference between the modern gloves and those old gloves of long ago allowed us to gain a great deal of respect for the fielding skills of those old players. The modern gloves were designed to trap the balls. Catching balls required little skill. Not so for the older gloves. They were essentially very thin pieces of leather sewed together. One had to use hands to trap the balls. Much greater skill was required. Catching with those gloves was not much different than catching with bare hands! It required a lot of courage to stick your hand out to catch a line drive. However, we were just glad to get some gloves. At one of our homecomings our track coach showed me a picture of the 1937 St. Louis Cardinals, along with a picture of us. Take away the faces and it would be hard to distinguish one from the other. Despite their problems, we wore the uniforms and used the gloves with pride. In hindsight, we had to be the coolest looking team ever!

In our very first practice, a tall child was chosen to throw practice pitches. We could not hit that ball! Our basketball coach remarked how inept we were and asked this tall kid to go further back, equivalent to the second base. Perhaps the coach believed this would give us more time to react to the pitch. We still could not hit the ball! I heard the basketball coach talking with the track coach. The basketball coach indicated we did not have anyone who could hit the ball. The older and wiser track coach replied that either we could not hit the ball, or the one throwing the ball was one hell of a pitcher. Thank God, the latter was the case. However, this was not realized until his senior year. If it had not been for our poor fielding that year, he would have pitched several no hitters.

During our first practice, we were sent out to shag fly balls. Our best athlete was given a small, thin bat to hit the balls to us. He was rarely successful in hitting the ball. When he did, it was not close to us. We found ourselves running and diving in attempts to catch them. In hindsight, this was probably good practice. Our assistant coach was long ago a baseball coach. In an act of extreme mercy, he took over that task of hitting fly balls to us. We soon discovered the difference in heights achieved by those hard balls and those by our softballs. Our inexperience in judging where they would come down resulted in the same diving exercise as before. Our efforts were certainly very serious, but could easily make the blooper highlights. Eventually many of us started laughing at our efforts. I must have been laughing too hard. My teammates approached me and threatened me with physical harm for laughing. I laughed harder, curled up in a ball, and laughed even harder as they pounded on me.

After several days of practice, we were given the good news. Our head coach confessed he had never coached a baseball team. That made us even! We had never played organized hard ball! There was even more good news. We were informed that a practice game was arranged with a nearby school. It was a school we knew all too well. Many children in that school had parents who worked at the home. While visiting, they bragged about the successes of their sports teams. Baseball was one game they enjoyed much success. We were somewhat apprehensive about playing such a good team, but we never backed down from challenges. The game was on. Based on our attire, it was like the 1937 Cardinals playing the 1956 Yankees. Based on our skill level and knowledge of the game, it was like our high school playing the 1956 Yankees. If choosing this school was an attempt to teach us the hard way, no pun intended, it was a rousing success. How rousing would be illustrated by the first two innings of organized ball we played.

My first observation was we had a real umpire. Wow! In sandlot ball, we normally played under the understanding that he who complained the loudest, or was the biggest, or the meanest, made the correct decisions. For example, calling strikes and balls; and deciding whether one was safe or out. Now we had an arbitrator. It was an answer from heaven to many of we small ones. Our first pitcher walked the first batter, the second, and then the third. He would have continued that forever if not for some unfortunate advice from you know who. He had the most amazing pitch. If he could control it, he would certainly become famous as a professional baseball player. The ball came up to the plate, took a dive, and faded very quickly to the right or to the left. Unfortunately, he had no idea how to control that pitch. He asked me for advice. I showed him how to throw the ball with the seams, helping to keep a straight line. With that advice, he served up a grand slam on the very next pitch. He never again asked me for advice, and I never volunteered any. Our next pitcher transformed a batter into a runner on four straight pitches. He then attempted to pick off that runner from first, from second, and finally from third. He was called for three straight balks, resulting in the first run for the opposing team. The umpire approached the mound, called over our coach, and requested him to demonstrate to our pitcher how to avoid balks. We had something to celebrate as the next batter was struck out!

To celebrate an out, our catcher proceeded to toss the ball around the horn, just like the tradition of professional teams. The first toss went over the first baseman's head into the pasture, meeting a fate all fear when venturing into that domain. After retrieving and wiping off the ball, it was tossed so far from the second baseman that he had to dive to stop it from being lost in the outfield. The second baseman managed to hit the shortstop in the back while tossing it to third base. The shortstop tossed it to the third baseman. Those familiar with this around-the-horn celebration know the ball then had to go to the pitcher. Our third baseman thought otherwise. He just had to get the outfield involved. The ball was tossed to me in left field, to center field, then to right field. Somehow, it finally made its way to the pitcher. During this celebration, the opposing team and umpire were very observant, and very quiet, surely astonished at the extent of this celebration. I noticed the umpire with his hands on his hips, shaking his head in disbelief.

The next batter got on base easily, complements of the umpire of course. A valuable lesson was learned about questioning his decisions. Our pitcher walked up to the mound and asked the umpire to dust off the plate.

The umpire said "I'm sorry, I didn't realize you couldn't see the plate."

Our pitcher responded, "I can see it fine."

Our substituted pitcher, the leader of the secret society, thought he was the cat's meow on presenting the ball to the batter. Was he wrong! The next batter hit the ball so far that I swear there were oohs from everyone, including our team. Fortunately, I had predicted where those balls would end up, which was far from where they were hit. To the surprise of all, including myself, I caught it! Everyone, including the opposite team, cheered! In keeping with our custom tradition of celebrating an out, I tossed the ball to the center fielder, who tossed it to the right fielder, then to the first baseman, then to the second baseman, then to the shortstop, then to the third baseman, and finally back to the pitcher. During this celebration, the runner that had walked tagged first base, cautiously made his way to second, then realizing what we were doing, ran to third and finally home. I noticed the umpire again shaking his head in disbelief. He again approached the pitching mound, then signaled the opposing team's coach, our coach, and all of us, for a meeting. He then told our coach to please explain when and how we should toss the ball around the horn to celebrate an out. The opposing team's coach must have felt sorry for us. He told his runner to go back to first base.

The bad news is that the other team managed to score so many runs that I swear we and they stopped counting. The good news is that we got plenty of fielding practice. All bad and good things come to an end. We got up to bat. What followed illustrated our ignorance of strategy involved in baseball. Perhaps we should have watched TV? Our first batter walked, an encouragement. To our dismay, he was called out on the hidden ball trick. At that time, we believed this was simply a dirty trick and not legal. I was the next at bat. Being short proved somewhat advantageous. The pitcher had a hard time with the strike zone. I was awarded first base on balls. I told the first baseman with the utmost confidence that I would not fall for that hidden ball trick. The pitcher started his windup, and I took a few steps off first. A whistle from the first baseman caught my attention. I glanced over. He was holding the ball!

What now followed illustrated our coach's failure to face reality, and our abilities to recognize it. Darkness and supper time were rapidly approaching. Our coach decided it was time for a pep talk. He was very good at pep talks, and we always responded with enthusiasm. With each statement of encouragement, I could feel the adrenaline increasing. We shouted to each other, offering encouragement to kick some butt. He made one tiny mistake. He reminded us how far we were behind, and told us we could start playing like he knew we could, or just go to dinner. We glanced at each other, realizing we were all thinking the same. We started walking back to our divisions to await the dinner bell. The coach started yelling that we could not quit, followed with some choice profanities. When I recall this game, I believe the children had a better grasp on reality than the coach.

THE HOOSIER 'GAME'

During my freshman year, our varsity basketball was comprised almost entirely of seniors. They had experience and talent, ingredients for a good year. When they all graduated, there were no experienced players for the next year's team. The local newspapers recognized this, reporting it would be a long year for Morton basketball, or possibly the first losing year for a very long time. Their expectations were accurate. The Indianapolis Star made it a point to publish a report that we had lost all the games played, which was a rarity. However disappointing that year was, it turned out to be one of my most memorable years. Several of these memories follow.

THE ENTREPRENEUR

With all the experienced seniors now graduated, even us more inexperienced players made the team the next year. We sophomores, the least experienced, sat on the bench, far from the coach. There was no chance in hell to get into a game. I did; the benefactor of an entrepreneur, with a capital E.

We players were welcome to free candy bars and popcorn from the refreshment stand. Before the game, several of us got candy and gave them to our entrepreneur. He then sold them at a discount during half-time. We split the profits. The candy he could not sell was hidden inside his jock while sitting on the bench. Any candy left over was sold during the next game. We never ate any of that candy, for obvious reasons. During one game, few people attended. He ended up with much more candy than normal in his jock. As we were sitting on the bench enjoying the game and the cheerleaders, our coach become fed up with the team's efforts to advance the ball over the half court line within the allocated ten seconds. In desperation, he made his way to the end of the bench, looking for someone that could dribble a basketball. His look of desperation made us believe that one of us would get to play. Some of us glanced at the ceiling, to the side, and in back, horrified we would be chosen. Some others were biting at the bit. I could swear coach said, "I don't believe I am doing this."

He pointed at our entrepreneur, saying, "I need someone that can get the ball over the ten second line. Can you do that."

Our entrepreneur was so excited, he yelled, "I can do that.:

He took off his jacket and ran out on the floor. We all yelled, excited one of us got a chance to play. Our entrepreneur was so excited, he forgot about the loot within his jock. When he reached center court, he realized the obvious bulges in his attire. He turned around and ran back to the coach. In sight of everyone he reached down into his jock, removed some candy, and handed it to the coach. After several repetitions of this he made the request "Hold these for me coach." He then ran back into the game. Our coach angrily threw the candy towards our bench, went onto the court, grabbed him by his jersey, and escorted him back to the bench where we were sitting.

We had to be serious about playing that which Hoosiers worship. However, some events are so funny that one cannot help but laugh. Coach noticed me doubling over about what had happened. He looked at me in disgust for so long that the officials came over and reminded him that he had to make a substitution. Coach then shook his head in what appeared to be another one of those "I don't believe I am doing this." looks.

He said "You think this is so funny. You go in and try it (get the ball over the ten second line)."

While talent is not an attribute I could brag about, dribbling the basketball was one I could. I had honed my dribbling talents trying to navigate the bulges in the floor at Town Hall, practicing, to attain that Hoosier dream. Advancing the ball beyond the half court line was a piece of cake. I saw plenty of playing time that year. Thanks to our entrepreneur.

OUR STAFF'S ENCOURAGEMENTS

We were taking a beating during the season. It would be the worst year in Morton's history for basketball. After each game, our coach, a former all-America basketball player convinced us to forge ahead, to win the next one. On we went to the next game, and the next, and the next, always expecting to win. Our coach never knew the meaning of quit. He saw that we were ready to give up. He decided to pull out all the stops to win the next game. Three strategies were devised, all which caused some unforgettable memories.

The entire home staff got involved with coach's first attempt to pick up our spirits. They arranged a basketball game, pitting the home staff against our basketball team. It was a very, very serious game. (LOL)

The governesses dressed up in cheer leader uniforms, all that fell short of hiding all they had. The uniforms were of all conceivable colors and patterns. Their skirts were far shorter than what our cheer leaders wore. It was obvious that age had solved that problem of modesty. Normally, the shorter the skirt, the better. I am not sure this applied in this case. The stark differences between them and our young, shapely, tight skin, small butt, cheer leaders was far funnier than what any blooper reel could show. Our wonderful governesses created wonderful, extremely funny, gut busting cheers. Without modesty, they kicked their legs high in the air, many times falling on their butts. Their underwear and bras appeared to be something you would see in a French house of ill repute. To say they acted in harmony like our real cheer leaders would be an injustice. When they gyrated their bodies like our cheer leaders, they ended up on the floor. Some attempted to do the splits, making it down about one quarter of the way. Skin was hanging from almost all areas, and their butts seemed enormous, compliments of pillows stuffed into their underwear. Some things you just got to see, to believe.

The staff men may have once been basketball players. It was obvious that was long ago. Like the governesses, they wore uniforms of different colors and patterns. Their shirts appeared to be from their high school. Their pants most certainly were not. Try to picture your Dad in his high school uniform. The skin of some seemed to be hanging from parts of their body. Most noticeable was that while their bodies changed direction, their skin did not. Their butts were enormous, although not from stuffing their underwear with pillows. Most obvious and funny was their stomachs; surely far different than the high school years. All parts of their bodies bounced as they ran, or most accurately, walked, down the floor. They were quite serious at winning the game. That seriousness, and their belief they could still accomplish what they obviously lost years ago, made their antics funnier. The fattest one on their team was the high scorer, compliments of the inability to move him from the center. It was one of those events that was very short, but would last a life time. You had to give the home staff straight A's in their efforts to pick up our spirits. Such wonderful people!

LOCKER ROOM ANTICS - SURPRISE

Our coach's next strategy to pick up our spirits will soon become evident. Locker-room antics were just as popular to us jocks as playing basketball. I apologize to all Hoosiers for saying that. In one antic, Jerry had on only his jock. He stretched one side over his shoulder, held his arms by his side like an ape, and made monkey noises. He looked like an ape man from the Stone Age! Everyone dittoed that and we jumped around the locker room acting stupid and laughing. Jerry and I had earlier talked with the coach in the gym, recognizing one of his strategies to encourage us to try harder. This will be revealed later. As we were hopping around making those ape sounds, I could see the wheels turning in Jerry's head. We had been partners in crime many times, and he drafted me for one more. The success of what he planned was contingent on whether the other players knew about our coach's strategy to encourage us. Apparently, they did not know.

As we participated in the antics of simulating caveman and monkeys, Jerry suggested we surprise coach by running out in the gym and performing those same antics. Everyone enthusiastically agreed. We all lined up against the outside wall of the gym and prepared our jocks. With those jocks pulled over our shoulder, our personal equipment was in clear view. Jerry volunteered to open the door to the gym while I stood at the end of the line. I had appropriated one of those brooms used to brush the gym floor. Out ran the team into the gym, all looking as ridiculous as ridiculous can be, making those monkey sounds. Once all were inside the gym, the door was closed and the broom placed across the handle so it could not be reopened from the gym side. Our dear friends would have to traverse the entire gym floor to escape out the other door. The strategy implemented by the coach to encourage us, unknown to the others, was to invite the governesses and teachers to watch us practice. Hearing the screams of the governesses, the coach, and then those of our dear friends was precious. Normally, we would have been hounded for life by the older boys. Fortunately, they did not realize who went out on the floor and who did not. Silence!

THE FINAL ATTEMPT

The last strategy used by the coach in a desperate attempt to make us winners was to arrange a special pep rally. We were to play against a school Morton had previously never played. We knew absolutely nothing about this school. We will call the team Sandusky. We had a popular cheer liked by all. It went something like, "Clap your hands" (everyone clapped their hands three times), "Stomp your feet" (everyone stomped their feet three times), "Beat those (mascot name)."

Carrie shared the enthusiasm of our coach. She always forged ahead, regardless of setbacks. The cheerleaders started that popular cheer.

They yelled "Clap your hands", upon which everyone clapped three times.

"Stomp your feet," upon which everyone stomped their feet three times.

"Beat those...", after which there was complete silence! No one had bothered to find out the name of the mascot! Without hesitation Carrie did not hesitate.

She again stomped her feet three times and yelled, "Beat those Sanduskians."

The entire student body and team were stunned. They were initially silent. To my surprise, they all joined Carrie and yelled "Beat those Sanduskians."

That battle cry of Carrie, paid dividends. We won the game! It was the only game we won that year. Every time I watch a sport when a team overcomes considerable difficulties to win the day, I recall that battle cry "Beat those Sanduskians."

33

A Memorable Walk

I learned some valuable lessons from my last serious incident at the home. It showed me the human side of home staff and taught me a lesson about violence. It also resulted in a walk to remember.

I was now in Division 27, reserved for seniors and juniors. I visited a friend in Division 28; next door. His governess ordered me to leave. I told her I wanted to tell my friend something, and held my hand up in that universal signal to wait. The governess hauled back and slapped me. I might add with an excellent right hand. In a knee-jerk reaction, I slapped her back. I quickly realized my stupidity and desperately tried to apologize. She grabbed the opposite end of an old, wood umbrella and proceeded to pound on my head with the wooden handle. Unfortunately, those old umbrellas were very sturdy, built from solid wood. I ran for my division. She followed and made mincemeat out of my head on the way. I made it inside the division. She followed and continued swinging that umbrella. The last view I had was her holding that umbrella like a baseball bat, swinging away. The umbrella was in shreds, most which were embedded into my head. I blacked out. When I gained my senses,

I discovered blood, lots of blood, on my head and on the floor. I was alone as everyone had left for supper. I tried to get up, but slipped on the considerable amount of blood on the floor. Heads bleed a lot! I made my way to a large double sink and held my head under the faucet. I became nauseated by the sight of blood washing down the drain. My head would not stop bleeding! I spent considerable time removing parts of the umbrella from my scalp. Each piece removed prompted more bleeding. The top of my head was absent of hair, something I can say does not bother me nowadays. After I had removed all embedded in my head, I had this urge to mop up the blood on the floor. I fainted dead away when I rung the mop out with my hands into the sink. I again gained my senses, put a towel over my head, and laid on the couch.

Everyone returned from supper. My governess must have learned what had happened. She mentioned that I was about to find out what happens when a home staffer is attacked. I realized that meant to be kicked out of the home. Later I found myself falling asleep on the couch. My governess told me to go to the hospital. I told her I was just tired, and went upstairs to bed.

During the middle of the night, I was wakened by one of the home staff. He first asked what happened to my head. I lied and told him I had fallen. After all, we children never told, never! He took me downstairs and advised that I had to leave the home for attacking one of its staff. I would have to leave in the morning. I never argued, and I never waited till morning. I retrieved my winter coat and left the division. The home staffer followed, repeating I should wait till morning. I ignored him. I walked down the brick road behind the boy's divisions, leading out of the home.

It was an extremely bright moonlit night. I could easily see my surroundings. I walked past the muddy field where the annual mud football game was played. I could see the seniors and underclassmen playing football that had no rules, and required no skills. I could see we children playing our version of that game; Mishawaka Football. I passed by Division 14. I could see hear our governess screaming as she watched Friday night wrestling. I could hear her bellowing out the words to that

Marine Air Force song "Off we go, into the wild blue yonder." Such good memories. I came upon Divisions 10 and 11 where the once "colored children" once stayed. I could now laugh at that characterization. I walked by the now unused, very small baseball diamond where extreme baseball was played. I saw myself in right field, next to the swings that ended my participation in that game. Ouch! I came upon Division 9. I could see Horse, his head held high, his mane and fur shiny like a new penny. I saw the young farm hand climbing down from the roof. I noticed the pretty young governess waving at him from her window. I remembered our wonderful governess that met that painful death. A sadness came over me. A short distance away was the muddy end of Lake Graham. I gave Fred a salute. "What a frog"! I came upon the old playground for Division 25. I remembered how little it was used. It was an age when our imaginations were much better for playing. I walked by Division 25 and glanced up at the window leading to the attic. The bats had long left for the night. I continued down the road where we toddlers in Division 25 had decided to run away. I laughed at that effort. I went by the store room where I had stolen, oops, I mean borrowed, items in a futile attempt at running away. At the end of that road I glanced over to the Jack and Jill park. I could see the adults laughing and pointing at toddlers splashing in that small cement wading pool. I stopped by our swimming hole in Lake Graham. I saw us stupid ones performing those stupid antics, attempting to amuse the girls. I noticed my Hollywood siblings on the diving board, trying to impress the same girls. I went by the water fall, into which I had fallen as a toddler. Ouch! I came upon the Girl's divisions. I could see those Guardian Angels sitting on those large cement porches. They smiled and waved, just as they had done when we very small children entered the home. I saw that special place I had spent as a four-year old. I once again heard Mom sing that lullaby. It was the most difficult remembrance of that walk. I came upon the old hospital; the first building I entered upon coming to the home. I could see those wonderful blue-tinged, uneven windows, and the vines that had climbed up to the roof. I reached the highway. Across it I could see the greenhouse where I spent most of my years. Behind that greenhouse was

Sadie. Though I could not see her, she was surely crying as we parted. I saw the old power plant where that annoying whistle barked out orders. I heard myself saying "If only I could get my hands around the neck of he who invented that whistle." I started down the highway. I went by the old graveyard where I ended up while playing that ridiculous but life-saving game "running thru the woods." I came upon the last remembrance of my home. It was an old highway sign "The Indiana Soldiers and Sailors Children's Home." The clouds now had ensured a dark night. It was as if I had left one world and entered one very different and unknown. As I continued, I felt that feeling of déjà vu leaving my body. As strange as it seems, I felt more elated the further from the home I got. It was as if heavy memories were being lifted from my shoulders. I came upon the old bridge over the Big Blue River. I remembered the old fishing hole underneath that bridge. Before crossing, I glanced back to see if any cars were coming. I remembered that we children would close our eyes as the enforcer drove the bus over that old bridge. It was so narrow that it was virtually impossible for two cars to safely pass by each other. I came upon two or three children hanging out in their front yard. They asked who I was. I answered. One of them recognized me from my basketball efforts against their team. He asked if I was the guard on that team from the home. I confirmed that I was indeed that person. They asked where I was going. I thought for a while, then answered "home." They were quiet momentarily. One of them said "Aren't you going the wrong way"? I answered "no". I continued towards the bus station in that small town.

A short time later the person that had told me they had to kick me out of the home drove up. He asked where I was going. I told him I was going to the bus station and then Indy. I had some relatives there. He offered, and I accepted, a ride to the bus station. The bus station was closed. I sat on the sidewalk outside the station, retrieved a hat from my coat, and put it on. This man again explained how ridiculous it was for me to insist on leaving that night. I ignored him. He offered some money from his own pocket for the bus ticket. He explained it was enough to get me to Indy. I had enough money for a ticket, but took the money anyway. He finally left.

Just as the sun was making its appearance, so did this man. He explained that he had asked others about the incident. Their version was very different than what the governesses had related. He asked me to come back to the home and stay until they could "straighten it out." I told him that I appreciated what the home had done for me, but I wanted nothing else. He stayed with me for some time, seemingly contemplating what to do. I paid for the ticket to Indy. Just as the bus arrived, this home staffer stopped me. He said something to the effect that they could fire him if them wanted to. He told me that I could stay at the home and graduate. That word "graduate" had significance. I knew the importance of a high school degree in getting a job. I agreed to go back to the home."

I was punished for slapping the governess. I could not participate in any activities, including Town Hall. Sports was the only exception. I apologized to the governess for slapping her. She never apologized for slapping me. Nor did she apologize for beating me with that umbrella. This incident showed the inhuman side of both her and I. We both resorted to violence. It also illustrated the human side of the home staffer. He took a big chance to allow me to continue in the home after slapping a governess. Regardless, it was a walk filled with remembrances of my time in the home.

34

I Am Not Myself

Like jigsaw puzzles, we spend a lifetime finding pieces that define our whole. Unlike puzzles, it is one that can never be completed. Pieces are found that fit. Those that once fit are removed, replaced with others. Pieces are borrowed from parents, mentors, teachers, and our own life experiences. For many homies, pieces that should come from parents and mentors were missing. Many found these pieces from unusual sources; the other children. With so many children, it was inevitable that one or more exceled in a specific aspect. They would provide missing puzzle pieces for others. I was the fortunate recipient of many such pieces. For the remainder of my life, I found it humorous when complemented on a piece of my puzzle. I would say to myself "That would be Frank", or whoever I used to create that piece.

35

Together Forever

The state closed the home. Its fate could have been predicted from the changes of the home over the years. The first sign was the fate of those wonderful, huge trees. They were all cut down. I participated in that distasteful crime, one of my many regrets. Later, six of the divisions were demolished, a sure sign fewer children needed the care of the home. Still later, more divisions disappeared. There was some encouragement the home would be continued. The old and failing activity center, Town Hall, was replaced with a new center. Losing that we cherished to much was so emotional to many that part of the old Town Hall was saved. It can still be seen with the newly constructed activity center. Many welcomed the birth of the new center, especially those that sought that Hoosier dream. The gym now had an official size floor, the hoops were regulation height, and there were no bulges in the gym floor. I accepted the fate that the home would face when it was discovered one I adored so much was no more. That wonderful Walnut tree in Spring Valley, the one I felt a kinship when first entering the home, was removed. Spared was its old friend, that Civil War theatre.

The reasons to close the home seemed to be many. It appeared when one reason was debunked, another was offered. There were efforts to save it, initiated by the children themselves and that wonderful organization that made sure no child was forgot. Regardless of what the state says, without a doubt the reason to close the home was the cost. Leave it to those in power to put a cost on the lives of children.

The home is no more for us that grew up in the Indiana Soldiers and Sailors Children's Home. It still lives in our thoughts. Thankfully, it still is a home. Sorely needed during this era is a school dedicated to giving children a second chance; those who cut their education short of a high school degree. They now have that second chance, owed to the mission of that we once called home.

These were memories of one child who found himself in the Indiana Soldiers and Sailors Children's home. There are thousands of other children with many more thousands of memories. They are stories of children thrown together in a state institution that provided care and opportunities when there were none. They are stories of virtual siblings, children whose kinships were kindled by togetherness. Through this togetherness, they developed a love for one another and a love for the home in which they lived. The home returned that love, manifested in the care and opportunities it provided. The benefactors were veterans of the civil war, their children, the children of veterans from other wars, orphans, and at-risk children. These benefactors will forever be in debt to the state for its efforts. Like all that ever was and is, the home has ended its worldly existence. However, it will live forever in the hearts and memories of the home children and their children. Our numbers grow less, victims of that fate of fates. As with Mom's lullaby, our memories of the time spent together are fading, soon to be no more.

When the time comes to journey to our final resident, we will once again briefly pass through our home. During that time we will eat together, play together, sleep together, attend the same school together, run through the same woods together, swim in that same swimming hole together, fish in Lake Graham together, search for Easter eggs not carefully hidden by our overseers, sleep, oops, I mean pray, in the same wonderful, Civil-War-era theatre together, tolerate the same timely whistles together, rub coat on those same old wooden floors together, march to the same old Civil War grave site together, dance to the tune of the Mortonairres together, make those Tigers proud together, and many other "togethers." These many "togethers" made us homies a family. When it is my turn, I believe the spirits of those homies proceeding me will be waiting with open arms, as I will for those that will come later. We will once again be together, as we were during our years at the home